SARAH B]
OF ST PETE

Sarah Biller (St Petersburg, probably late 1840s).

For Jeanne

Sarah Biller
of St Petersburg

A Sheffield Teacher in
19th Century Russia

JOHN DUNSTAN

*from John
with best wishes*

25 July 2013

William Sessions Limited
York, England

ISBN 978-1-85072-399-8

Printed in 10 on 11 point Plantin
from Author's Disc
by Sessions of York
The Ebor Press
York, England

CONTENTS

NOTE ON ILLUSTRATIONS

The unique portrait of Sarah Biller and images of the Community of Sisters of Charity, whose first director she was, originally appeared in a book marking its 50th anniversary: *Istoricheskii ocherk Svyato-Troitskoi Obshchiny sestër miloserdiya v S.-Peterburge za pyatidesyatiletie 1844-1894.* I am very grateful indeed to the Russian Academy of Sciences Library, St Petersburg, the owner of the book, for making them available.

No picture of Sarah in her Kilham days seems to exist, but the gap has been imaginatively filled by Brenda Tyler, and she retains copyright of the line drawings.

The sketch of Alexander Kilham is taken from W.J. Townsend, *Alexander Kilham, the First Methodist Reformer* (London, [1889]); the drawing of the Lord's House is from A. Gatty, *Sheffield Past and Present* (Sheffield, 1873); and the map of part of Sarah's Sheffield is from John Leather's 'Plan of Sheffield in 1823'. Thanks go to the Local Studies Service, Sheffield Central Library for supplying them for my use.

The three portraits of Russian notables were published in various issues of the journal *Russkaya starina.* They appear by courtesy of the University Library at the University of Sheffield.

The plan of St Petersburg in 1849 was drawn by N. Tsylov and reproduced by E. Lopatina (1959). It appears by courtesy of the Alexander Baykov Library, European Resource Centre, University of Birmingham.

The photographs taken at Pickering in and around the Parish Church and in the garden of the Friends Meeting House at Evesham are the copyright of the author, who is grateful to the Pickering PCC and the Evesham Friends respectively.

PREFACE AND ACKNOWLEDGMENTS

THE ORIGINS of this book lie in a coincidence of reading matter over thirty years ago. I was researching residential education in the USSR and its antecedents in the imperial era; casting my net widely I landed *Quakers in Russia* by Richenda Scott. She devoted two pages to a young Sheffield woman who arrived in St Petersburg in 1820 to start a school there.[1] Her name was Sarah Kilham, and she was the step-daughter of Hannah, a pioneer of education in West Africa. Whether this rang a faint bell I cannot remember, but one certainly sounded loud and clear from the next issue of the *Proceedings of the Wesley Historical Society*, where E.A. Rose pointed out in a note that Sarah was the only surviving child of Alexander Kilham,[2] leader of the first major schism in Methodism and co-founder of the Methodist New Connexion. As an adoptive Sheffielder I knew what used to be Scotland Street Chapel (1829) and its precursor's part in Methodist history.

Since then I have pursued Sarah Kilham with something of the doggedness of the Hound of Heaven: not so much down the nights and down the days as when time and serendipity permitted, but certainly down the arches of the years and down the labyrinthine ways of numerous libraries and archives. I should like to express my thanks to many archivists and librarians, particularly at Friends House Library, London, and also at the Alexander Baykov Library, European Resource Centre, University of Birmingham; Woodbrooke College, Birmingham; Bible Society Library, Cambridge University Library; British and Foreign Schools Society Archives Centre, Brunel University, Isleworth; Leeds Russian Archive, Brotherton Library, University of Leeds; Lincolnshire Records, Lincoln; Liverpool Record Office; British Library, London; Guildhall Library, London; National Portrait Gallery, London; Archives of Council for World Mission, School of Oriental and African Studies, London; Wellcome Library, London; Methodist Archives and Research Centre, The John Rylands University Library, Manchester; Archives and Local Studies, Manchester Central Library; Nottingham City Library; Quaker Meeting House Library, Sheffield; Sheffield Archives; Local Studies Service, Sheffield Central Library; Western Bank Library, University of Sheffield; Worcester History Centre; and North Yorkshire Record Office, Northallerton.

I wish also to thank Dr Natalia Kolpakova and Ms Anna Zhabreva of the Russian Academy of Sciences Library (BAN) in St Petersburg and Mr Yury Weisberg for facilitating the contact there. Before her thesis was published, Dr Julia Mahnke-Devlin (formerly of the Osteuropa-Institut in Munich) kindly shared with me some of her findings at the Russian

State Historical Archive in St Petersburg and the Main Archive of the Russian Federation, Moscow. I am also endebted to Mrs Helen Beaumont and Mr Stanley Johnson (Isle of Axholme Family History Society, Epworth), and am especially grateful to Mr Mike Berry (University of Birmingham) and Professor J.Y. Muckle (University of Nottingham).

As well as thanking the staff, I am happy to acknowledge permission for the use of manuscript sources in the four major English archives containing material directly on Sarah. Letters shedding light on her family background and childhood, housed at MARC, are cited with the permission of the Archives and History Committee of the Methodist Church of Great Britain and reproduced by courtesy of the University Librarian and Director of The John Rylands University Library, The University of Manchester. The circumstances of her arrival in St Petersburg and her earlier years there, along with occasional later events, are documented in letters held at The Library of the Religious Society of Friends (Friends House Library) in London. Materials illuminating the first half of her Russian career are reproduced from London Missionary Society/Council for World Mission Archives at SOAS, University of London. Slightly later correspondence overlapping this period is to be found in the Bible Society Library at Cambridge University Library.

In the lengthy course of my research I have moved from traditional means of genealogical study to modern ones (which is the reason for differing styles of census references) and I should like to acknowledge www.ancestrylibrary.com as a very convenient site. Another site, www.measuringworth.com, accomplishes the difficult task of expressing the purchasing power of the pound of long ago in terms meaningful for today. Three excellent Russian sites – www.citywalls.ru (history of buildings and their context), www.inform-t.ru (biography) and www.randd.ru (Parish of St Panteleimon, Orthodox Diocese of Novosibirsk) – have marshalled data otherwise impossible to find outside Russia.

A somewhat shorter version of chapter 1 has appeared as an article in the *Proceedings of the Wesley Historical Society*.[3] I am grateful to the Editor, Alan Rose, for his cooperation.

My two original sources said that there were 'tantalisingly few glimpses' (Scott) of Sarah and her 'astonishing career' (Rose). Three other writers in particular have helped to fill out specific aspects of her biography: Mora Dickson[4] has touched on her relationship as a young woman with her stepmother Hannah Kilham; Ormerod Greenwood[5] has supplemented Richenda Scott on the contemporary activities of her Quaker and other friends in St Petersburg; and much more recently Wendy Rosslyn[6] has depicted her and other British expatriates in their dealings with Russian philanthropists. She has also presented a new brief outline of Sarah's career, from sources which include fresh ones. My own purpose is to bring together as much as possible of the life-story of this elusive and self-effacing woman, setting it where appropriate in its wider context of historical developments and personal relationships, and to suggest some reasons why she deserves to be remembered.

John Dunstan
Sheffield, June 2009

Notes and References

1 R.C. Scott, *Quakers in Russia* (London, 1964), pp 92-4.
2 E.A. Rose, 'Sarah Kilham and Hannah Kilham', *Proceedings of the Wesley Historical Society [PWHS]*, 39 (1974), pp 185-6.
3 J.Dunstan, 'Alexander's Daughter: The Childhood of Sarah Kilham', *PWHS*, 56 (2008), pp 213-27.
4 M. Dickson, *The Powerful Bond: Hannah Kilham 1774-1832* (London, 1980).
5 J.O. Greenwood, *Quaker Encounters, 2: Vines on the Mountains* (York, 1977).
6 W. Rosslyn, 'Benevolent Ladies and their Exertions for the Good of Humankind: V.A. Repnina, S.S. Meshcherskaia. and the Origins of Female Philanthropy in Early Nineteenth-Century Russia', *Slavonic and East European Review*, 84 (2006), pp 52-82, and 'Women with a Mission: British Female Evangelicals in the Russian Empire in the Early Nineteenth Century', in W. Rosslyn and A. Tosi, ed., *Women in Russian Culture and Society 1700-1825* (Basingstoke and New York, 2007), pp 219-40.

1. FAMILY HISTORIES

SARAH'S BACKGROUND AND CHILDHOOD

The Kilhams of Epworth

FIFTY-NINE years after John Wesley was born, the small north-west Lincolnshire town of Epworth, through a seeming irony of Providence, was to see the birth of the principal leader of the first major secession from the movement that he founded. This was Alexander Kilham, who in 1797 would establish the Methodist New Connexion (MNC).[1] Our focus here is chiefly on the events in his life which would have some bearing on his daughter Sarah's, the hero of our story. Alexander was born on 10 July 1762 and baptised at St Andrew's Church on 6 August, the third son of Simon Kilham or Killam (1729-1802), a linen weaver, and Elizabeth, *née* Ingham; they had married in 1751. The eldest son was another Simon (1758-1836), the second Richard (born 1760) and the youngest Thomas (?1764-1826).[2] Alexander's actual birthplace cannot be pinpointed with absolute accuracy. There is, however, a tradition in Epworth that the Kilham family home was a former farm, now much changed and called Prospect House, otherwise 79 High Street. This is almost opposite Tottermire Lane and near the end of the long main street from the Market Cross.

Simon Kilham, our Sarah's grandfather, was the son of Richard, an Epworth blacksmith, who died when the boy was ten. Moving then to Crook House in the township of Darfield, east of Barnsley, to be brought up by an uncle, at about 17 he worked for a farmer for a year. Then he returned to Epworth as apprentice to his uncle, Samuel Crawshaw, to learn the weaver's trade. This was the start of the Kilhams' Methodist story, for Crawshaw was a member of Epworth's original Methodist society.[3] (John Wesley had met a group of followers there on his return to his home town in June 1742. This was after he had been barred from the church pulpit by a curate hostile to his Gospel preaching, and he had later stood outside on his father's tombstone to address a huge congregation.)[4] Travelling preachers were visiting the town. Simon began to attend the public preaching and soon afterwards the private meetings. He had had a childhood conversion experience, but receiving no encouragement he had grown slack. Now he was re-awakened and became a Methodist himself. His future wife Elizabeth, of Baptist origins, was also to join the society.

Alexander Kilham and his brothers received home schooling from their father: the three Rs plus religious instruction.

1

He taught us our duty to God and our neighbour, and often told us that God would love us if we feared and loved him. He took us to the church and Methodist meeting; he explained such things as we were willing to learn, caused us to read certain select passages of scripture, and bought us godly books, well knowing how pleasing variety is to the young.

He also told them about his own faith journey.[5] But they grew older, and to some extent rebelled. This culminated in a cock-fighting incident early in 1782, for which one of the boys (not named) helped himself to their father's bird. He reasoned with the culprit so effectively that none of them ever did it again. This seems to have been the first stage in a catalytic process that ended with the conversion of all four sons, for this was the period of the Epworth revival (1781-2) and children and young adults figured prominently in it. They included Alexander's three brothers and a sister-in-law,[6] probably Simon's new bride Mary.

Wesley refers to the wholesome effect of the revival upon three spinning and weaving factories where the young people worked.[7] Perhaps he included the small sacking manufactory which Simon senior had set up for his children's sake. Alexander's specialism was marketing the product, and he excelled at it.[8] He was the last of the brothers to convert,[9] but the only one whose conversion brought about a dramatic career change. He would remain an effective travelling salesman but the commodity became a spiritual one. He responded to the call progressively in private prayer meetings, public ones and a mission band; then he served as a local preacher and from 1783 as travelling aide of Squire Robert Carr Brackenbury in Gainsborough and the Channel Islands. Alexander's parents resisted this at first,[10] but they saw that God's will must be done. It meant sacrifices, not only of his company but also of the considerable business that he had brought to the family firm.[11]

Alexander Kilham's next five years need not detain us long: supplying the Grimsby Circuit full-time, being recommended to Wesley for the itinerancy by the supervising preacher there, and appointed successively to Horncastle (1785), Gainsborough (1786) and Scarborough (1787). (The Methodist 'circuit' was the area in which a travelling preacher made the rounds of the 'societies' entrusted to his care and did evangelistic work.) Less well-known perhaps is the fact that at Gainsborough in June 1787 Alexander fell ill from overwork and was sent to Hull to rest and recuperate. He apparently recovered, but it was reported to his mentor Squire Brackenbury that he had consumption (tuberculosis). Concern must have remained because a year later he enquired of William Warrener, Methodism's first missionary in Antigua, about the suitability of the West Indian climate for 'persons of a consumptive condition'. Despite an encouraging answer he did not pursue this, maybe for domestic reasons.[12]

Yet one cannot but speculate whether such a propensity would play a part in sad events some ten years on.

Alexander, Sarah and Sally

A credible domestic reason was that Alexander had found a wife. Let us hear in his own words how they met. A friend in the Scarborough Circuit had pointed out Sarah Gray (or Grey) to him.

> [He] told me he thought she would make me a proper companion, and supposed she would have no great objection to enter into my line of life. – As he spoke so warmly on this matter, and said so much in her favour, I was determined to see her, and laid the matter before the Lord, begging his direction. I accordingly paid her a visit, and finding her disengaged, and that she had no objection either to my person or line of life, an acquaintance began, and our union in a few months was the consequence of it.[13]

The visit was in December and they were married at Pickering Parish Church of St Peter and St Paul on Easter Monday, 24 March 1788, with Wesley's due permission.[14] Vitally, as Alexander was still within his 4-year period of probation, his bride's independent means enabled him to guarantee that Methodist Connexional funds would not be affected.[15]

Sarah was 32, born at Pickering on 9 October 1756 and baptised the next day, the daughter of John Gray, captain of an American merchantman, and Hannah.[16] The parish registers had recorded the marriage of John Gray of Scarborough and Hannah Lythe on 17 February 1736. The Lythes hailed from Newton, a few miles north of Pickering, but as no other place is stated we may assume that she was living in the town.[17]

In his extensive obituary of his wife, Alexander notes that she 'went to live' with a

Willowgate, Pickering. The cottage on the left, partly in shadow and now with drainpipe, is reputedly where Pickering's first Methodists met.

schoolmaster called Ellart; her mother gives the date of this as 1774.[18] Mr William Ellart, schoolmaster, was buried at Pickering on 8 August 1786.[19] From this we deduce that he had been working locally, but we have not discovered a connection with any known school or indeed found any reference to education for girls at this time. Nevertheless, Sarah seems to have had certain means of her own – probably inherited from her father, who according to Alexander died in America of a fever,[20] though he does not say when this was – so it is likely that she was a private pupil of Mr Ellart's, acquiring from him her polished style of letter-writing and perhaps assisting him in his work.

Sarah was converted under the ministry of an Anglican clergyman, Mr Robinson.[21] John Robinson was serving as curate at Pickering Parish Church in 1775 and as vicar from 1784 to 1786.[22] In 1785 she became a member of the Methodist society, joining Hannah who had been one of the original twelve at its formation in 1777. Sarah appeared in the membership rolls for the last time as Sarah Gray in 1787 and once only as Sarah Kilham in 1788.[23] John Blackwell describes her as eminently sensible, affectionate and caring. Her letters suggest also a lively sense of humour. Her husband wrote of her:

> I have frequently found my heart overwhelmed with gratitude and love to Him for giving me such a helpmate, for her whole study has been to glorify God and render herself agreeable to me... He has given me a partner in whom I find all the qualities I ever desired, and many others which I never looked for.[24]

Sarah had a house in Pickering and kept it up through Alexander's second year in the circuit. It was there that Sarah junior, whom we shall call Sally during her childhood, came into the world in December 1788. This is how Alexander recorded the happy event:

> I was now informed of my dear wife being safely delivered of a daughter, and of her being in a hopeful way; I immediately went home to see her: we rejoiced together, and solemnly offered up our infant to the Lord to be his for ever.[25]

Appropriately, for in many ways she took after him, it is her father who introduces us to the star of this story. She was baptised at the Parish Church on 24 May 1789, Alexander probably deferring to his wife and mother-in-law on this occasion, in contrast to a later event at Whitby.

We can stand in Pickering Market Place and picture the baby being brought for baptism. The church spire can be seen from miles around, yet the rest of the building can barely be glimpsed until we are almost upon it. It stands on an eminence but is hemmed in by houses, and we can reach it only by a narrow lane from the east or by flights of ancient stone stairs from the west, south-west and south. So we gain the

Pickering Parish Church: 14th century south porch.

Pickering Parish Church: Saxon font upon a later base.

churchyard, very soon to be faced with another flight of ten steps up to the south porch. These approaches must have been very familiar to Hannah Gray and Sarah but the church looked quite different inside. People sat in box pews at that time, and these are long gone. The most famous feature of today's building, however, remained treasure hidden from the Grays: the 15th-century wall paintings still lay forgotten under their coat of plaster. On the other hand, here before us is a direct connection, through Sally and her mother, with the Saxon predecessor of the Norman church that formed the core of the present one. This is the font,[26] originally low on the ground without its thick pillar so that people could step into it. It is moving to see and touch so close a link with our chief character as a very juvenile lead.

Sally, too young to remember, soon left Pickering and moved round the North with her parents: the next year to Pocklington and a tiny uncomfortable house in a huge circuit with a six-week preaching round; in 1790 to Whitby, where her brother Samuel was born in March 1791, provoking a dispute between their father and a leading local Methodist who demanded that he should be baptised in the Parish Church and his mother churched there;[27] and then to Newcastle-upon-Tyne, where he died in

November from inflammation of the chest: 'the Lord called us to part with our dear little boy', as his father put it.[28]

John Wesley had died on 2 March 1791. Early in the next year Alexander was in the public eye more than locally by circulating a pamphlet – the first of many on constitutional issues – defending his retired colleague Joseph Cownley for celebrating the Lord's Supper. It was later claimed that without his wife's money he could not have afforded to post his publications all over the kingdom.[29] The Conference – Methodism's governing body – of 1792, shunning a radical image in a revolutionary era, censured him and 'banished' him to Aberdeen as 'assistant', i.e. supervising preacher.[30] (Four years later, the still current title 'superintendent' would come into use.) Another step taken by that Conference was a ban on the newish and uncommon practice of ordination. Alexander had just been ordained by none other than Joseph Cownley (assisted by Charles Atmore).[31] It would not be surprising if some members of Conference regarded them as two trouble-makers in cahoots. Alexander had a capacity for presenting events in a personally favourable light: nobody wanted to go to Aberdeen, he later wrote, so he consented on condition that he and his family could stay in Newcastle until Sarah had recovered from her next confinement, and Conference agreed. It was another boy, another Samuel; this was a late example of the practice of naming a child after a deceased infant sibling. They moved to Aberdeen in October.[32]

The journey nevertheless proved very trying for Sarah and the baby, but the little girl, now nearly 4, was tougher. Alexander confirmed their safe arrival and warm welcome in a long letter to John Gaulter in Newcastle, describing the work already under way and also making the earliest references so far found to his daughter as a person in her own right: 'Sarah often talks about R—— and asks when she will come in the Coach'. He followed this with some very odd remarks about the Grays, presumably his in-laws, who had tracked them down to Aberdeen. 'They are pretty numerous. We treat them so badly and persecute them to death that we hope they will be tired of us & remove where they can be better used'.[33] This was, we may suppose, a jocular comment about relatives who he felt were trying to sponge off them.

Although Alexander Kilham enjoyed the opportunity afforded by his Aberdeen appointment to generate a profusion of reformist pamphlets, his satisfaction evidently came to be marred by other family problems. Perhaps the writing was literally a diversion. Ten months after arriving in Aberdeen, 'our second Samuel' died of the measles. It was too much for Sarah and she suffered recurrent breakdowns in health, psychological at least in part. There is a sad memento of this in the preachers' account book: Alexander recorded a grant of £2 5s 6d as 'Expences of the Child's funeral & the Dr. in my wife's late affliction'.[34]

For compassionate reasons the 1794 Conference permitted her husband to stay in Aberdeen for a third year, but circuit engagements continued to make their claims. Sarah encouraged him heroically, but for her unspoken feelings we must read between the lines of a comment by little Sally which she relayed to him: 'she says, I must be father and mother to her, since her father stays so long away'. Miscarriage followed miscarriage.[35] Alexander courted controversy and his frequent disputes could have done nothing for Sarah's peace of mind either. In 1795 they were to be transferred to Alnwick. About to leave her Scottish friends and with another rare reference to Sally, she wrote to Alexander, 'I hope the Lord will give me and the child strength to prosecute the journey'. They sailed to Shields for Alnwick, and she rallied.[36]

But it did not last long. Alexander's feeling of being surrounded by a host of foes was exacerbated by the publication of *The Progress of Liberty amongst the People called Methodists*, which Alan Rose calls 'his most strident pamphlet'.[37] On any foes within we can only speculate, but surely he was not impervious to his wife's troubled state. He was certainly aware of it. For the fateful Conference of 1796 Sarah rode with him and Sally to the circuit boundary. The horse became 'unruly' and she was forced to jump off, severely spraining her ankle. 'Under the protection of a good and gracious providence, I and my dear Sally got safe to Alnwick last night... in a return chaise', she wrote. She was too lame to leave the house. 'Sally is well and gives her love'.[38] Sally was now 7½ years old, quite capable of remembering such a dramatic incident, and there was worse to come. Yet in later life, in such of her own writings and accounts of her as have survived, there is never a word about this, and indeed very little about her mother. We may well surmise that it was just too painful to recall. Alexander, referring to the event in his journal, wrote of his wife: 'the recent hurt that she had received added to her dejection'.[39]

Riled by Alexander's personal attacks even more than his proposals for the democratization of Methodism's governmental structures at all levels, Conference expelled him. Sarah felt the turbulence in faraway Alnwick. 'The news is spreading through the town like fire', wrote Stephen Eversfield, the junior minister, on 30 July. She was too much affected to write then,[40] but in her next letter she expressed herself with unusual frankness:

> Language fails to tell thee of the distressing time we have had to pass through. I had many friends uniting to comfort me; others, that before appeared friendly, were rejoicing at our downfall.[41]

Later she recovered enough to write bravely:

> Poor George Ferguson was almost raving. He told Mr E the first preacher that came to his house when he was got to bed, he would

load a pistol and go to his bedside and say, were you one that lifted a hand against Mr K and then present the pistol to his head and make him beg pardon or blow his brains out. Amidst our sorrows we had many a hearty laugh at the various scenes that passed in different families.[42]

Sorrows there were aplenty. One expulsion led to another: mother and daughter had had to leave their Alnwick home. This was a logical outcome, but Alexander clearly felt that it had been done harshly. Fortunately there were offers of hospitality from friends, and Sarah and Sally moved successively to Newcastle, Sunderland, Pickering (doubtless to her mother's), Leeds and various places in what is now Greater Manchester. Meanwhile Alexander was producing his *Methodist Monitor*, campaigning and preaching in the North of England wherever he was welcome, and seeing his family at intervals.[43] In November he wrote from Liverpool that he had heard his wife was very poorly; ever since he had left Salford she had been confined to her room.[44]

Enervated by her nomadic life, in mid-January 1797 Sarah suffered the start of her final breakdown, characterized by violent headaches and stomach upsets leading to inability to eat. A pathetic bill from the doctor survives: embrocations for her head, a 'stomachic mixture' and injections of bark,[45] i.e. quinine, used to treat fever. For five weeks she wasted away until the end came on 23 February, at the house of William Heginbottom in Ashton-under-Lyne. She was 40 years old. Alexander preached at her funeral and on related themes at morning and evening services on the same Sunday.[46] Her burial place was Ashton churchyard.[47]

On hearing the sad news, Alexander's brother-in-law wrote to the widower, describing his reactions in unusually graphic language:

My Dearest Brother
    It is in tears that I write to you but hopes that the Lord will strengthen me in this heavy trial. The first news I got of my dear sister being dead was at Kingthorpe. I was in the attic storey of the Hall putting in some sashes and one of our boys came up to me and said Tommy, did you know that your sister is dead. I suddenly replied what sister, he said your sister Salley. I thought I should have fallen down betwixt the joists but I got off them as fast as I could for I did love my dear sister with [sic] to a very great degree... I desire to return you most humble thanks for what you sent me...
    I remain your Loving Brother
    Tho[s] Gray
Brother Ward's Love to you and Ann Skelton's, Brother King's and Brother Lotherington's, and they should all be very glad to see you.[48]

Kingthorpe is not quite 3 miles from Pickering along the Whitby road. The people named were all Methodists. Joseph King had led the Pickering society from the start.[49]

With Alexander's travelling campaign in full swing, what was to become of 8-year-old Sally? In their letters of sympathy both his mother-in-law and his father had alluded to their grandchild. Hannah Gray had written:

> My whole thoughts are taken up by thinking of you and my dear little Salley. I do assure you I and the rest of my family and many friends do feel much for you and I could wish if it is agreeable to you to send little Salley to my house, she should have every necessary comfort I could make her, but you being her father has [sic] the only right to do as you think the best.[50]

In fact Alexander had already exercised this right. He had written to his father, Simon Kilham, who fortunately had failed to fulfil his own prediction some 30 months earlier that he would 'see [his son's] face no more on this side of the grave',[51] asking if Sally might stay with him until the 1797 Conference. Simon, now 67 and since 1785 a widower, replied from Epworth on 28 February:

> I say bring her, she shall be as welcome as ever thou was for I long to see her. When thou sends I will meet thee at Doncaster with thy horse & another to bring her on & I think as we shall be all strange to her thou had better come on with us to my house & stay all night with her & next morning go on to Thorne for a few days & then come back & thou will see how she settles with us, for Beckey [his housekeeper?] will do the best she can for her & she is very well qualified, I think, as any body I know of for the same, and she will be glad to see her at our house, she shall want for nothing we can do for her.

He was sorry that he had not known how ill her mother was or he would have come over to Leeds one last time to see her. 'But it is all over now so let thy little lass come, let her go nowhere else'.[52] Simon's kindly thoughtfulness shines through.

Sally in Epworth

So Alexander took Sally with him to Barnsley, where he preached in the Independent chapel, met his father and brother at Doncaster and handed her over. But he was made of sterner stuff than his father. He stuck to his plan to proceed immediately to Thorne and preach in that area for a week before visiting Epworth, where on 1 April he completed his short biography of Sarah, with the three sermons appended. In this he tried, and forty years later Blackwell tried harder still, to refute the criticism that Sarah's tragic end was the result of his opposition to the Wesleyan preachers. Yet if that had been so, he argued, the direct cause had been his expulsion – and her subsequent eviction – by Conference. He stressed that during her troubles he had travelled only at her insistence.[53] We need not be judgmental, for even today anyone with a job to do and a sick spouse to support will empathize with Alexander in his dilemma. To be sure, his response to his father's suggestion about staying with Sally overnight shows a high degree of tough-mindedness. In recent months, however, the child had grown used to care by strangers, and perhaps she was already building upon an inherited resilience of character which would stand her in good stead in later years.

After his Epworth interlude, Alexander said good-bye to his daughter and returned to Leeds via the East and North Ridings.[54] Whatever his opinion of the other Grays, he evidently thought well of his mother-in-law Hannah. He visited her in Pickering, mourned Sarah with her, and called her 'a woman of real grace'. He preached in the chapel and found most people still well-disposed to him, a welcome contrast to his earlier reception in nearby Malton.[55]

In Epworth, we may assume, old Simon was still living on the family farm mentioned earlier, half a mile north-west of the Old Rectory. He had probably been joined by his eldest son and namesake, himself a widower with four young children and several more to come from a second marriage.[56] So Sally had no shortage of Epworth cousins, and it was this uncle with whom she kept in touch in later life. Simon and his father were both paying land tax in 1795, and by 1800 they had been joined in the assessments by the other two brothers, Richard and Thomas, a clockmaker.[57] This suggests a modest prospering of the family fortunes.

On 9 May, about a month after Alexander's departure from Epworth, his father sent him a letter partly on the business of the forthcoming Conference and partly on personal matters in which Sally figures prominently. She and Rebeccah send thanks for their presents. She is very content and happy and keeps as 'close' to her reading, writing, knitting and sewing as they can expect. Simon also reports an intriguing comment by Sally: 'she says she is at home and she will not leave her Grandfather, no not at Conference but thou must remember she is but a child'. We recall that Simon invited Sally to stay with him until the next Conference. Above and beyond that, given the 8-year-old's experiences, we might well conclude that she has at last found a stable environment but associates the word 'Conference' with disruption and trouble.

There is also a hint that Alexander has been sounding Simon out on remarriage: he is at liberty to marry again, the old man writes, only let him do the Lord's will. Then follows something unique: a short note from

Sally herself, sandwiched between her grandfather's news and views, in a bold but somewhat irregular hand:

> Hon^rd and dear Father I received your kind advice And am glad to hear from you and that you are in health let me hear from you again as soon as you can. Sarah Kilham.[58]

The salutation seems to show a mixture of formality and affection in the little girl's relationship with her father, at a time when the pendulum was starting to swing back to the deference of two centuries earlier.[59] What the letter does not reveal is much of Sally herself. The child is mother of the woman.

This was the period when Sally had her only protracted experience of Epworth Methodism, for she stayed at her grandfather's until April 1798. She would have known the earliest chapel there, for which Frank Baker tracked down the Dissenters' Certificate of 1772 signed by Thomas Lee and referring to their intention 'to make use of the lately erected building (commonly called the Preaching-house) situate in Epworth... as a place of Publick Worship of Almighty God'.[60] She would also have been a somewhat uncomprehending witness to the local impact of Methodism's first significant schism. Rose provides an account of the separation: Alexander's failure to persuade the 1797 Conference to accept lay representation; the inauguration of the 'New Itinerancy' at Ebenezer Chapel, Leeds, by himself as Secretary, three other preachers – William Thom, elected first President, the loyal Stephen Eversfield from Alnwick, and Alexander Cummin – and a small group of laymen; and the defection of some 5,000 members (5%) from the Wesleyans.[61] The Kilham family at Epworth naturally supported their famous – or notorious – kinsman.[62]

In case these repeated references to 'Conference' are confusing, especially in and after 1797, let us pause to demystify them. When the three preachers withdrew from the Methodist Conference to meet with Alexander and others and found the New Connexion on 9 August 1797, they were in effect holding an independent Conference. From then on there were *two* annual Conferences, that of the parent Wesleyan body and that of its rebellious MNC offspring, until further secessions added to their number.

We began this chapter by calling Alexander the *principal* founder of the MNC as his unique ascription to that role has been hotly contested.[63] He was the impetuous, fiery reformer who saw himself as a revolutionary; William Thom was the careful, thoughtful administrator and planner. Thumbnail sketches by a contemporary Wesleyan critic present the former as 'fractious' and 'fond of controversy', the latter as 'sensible and pious, a man of considerable learning – but a dull, unpopular preacher'.[64] There

Alexander Kilham (from Townsend).

can, however, be no doubt that Alexander was the driving force, so perhaps we should be just as single-minded and give him his full due.

As for the chapels, the New Connexion normally had to provide its own, although in about a dozen cases with a majority of sympathetic trustees the seceders appropriated the buildings, at least temporarily, as at Hockley in Nottingham. At Epworth, however, the situation was almost unique: it was one of three chapels shared between the two Connexions, probably each providing preachers every other Sunday. How much goodwill was there on both sides in this community, and how well did it mix with *force majeure* on the Kilhamite side and acceptance among the Wesleyans? Kilhamite supporters predominated in the trust. In 1797 legal advice was taken on the deeds and in 1798 Alexander actually tried to have the building legally transferred.[65] He did not succeed, but if made public this would surely have been perceived as a hostile act. It says much at least for mutual tolerance that the arrangement continued for some six years; but at length the New Connexion people had to quit. Not surprisingly, one of their partisans would blame the Wesleyans: 'a spirit not commendable was manifested by the leading friends in the Old [Connexion]'.[66] For the present, like her father in his day, but now in a highly politicized atmosphere, Sally was witness to a succession of preachers enjoying the hospitality of the Kilhams.[67]

Hannah Spurr of Sheffield

Meanwhile, in Sheffield, events were unfolding which would bring about a formative force in Sally's life and a defining influence on her career. The founding Conference of the MNC on 9 August 1797 named Sheffield first in the list of places where they had supporters,[68] and appointed Alexander there. On the same day Hannah Spurr, nearly 23, wrote in her occasional journal about the schismatics of whom she had just heard:

> Who are these poor Kilhamites (as they are called), so despised by some, and pitied by others? They are immortal souls – they are not contemptible – not beneath our notice! Oh, God, direct me![69]

As the future Hannah Kilham has been the subject of a substantial modern biography – Mora Dickson's *The Powerful Bond* (1980) – details here will be sparing, except in so far as they relate to her stepdaughter and apart from some newly-found references.

Briefly to sketch Hannah's childhood and youth: she was born on 12 August 1774, the seventh child of Peter and Hannah Spurr, 'respectable tradespeople'. Hannah senior was described as 'a woman of keen intellect, stainless life, and devout spirit'.[70] Peter was born in 1735, apprenticed in 1748, received his freedom in 1758, married in 1762 and became Master Cutler in 1781.[71] According to Sarah they were 'of modest means'.[72] In 1779 Peter Spurr was renting his premises from the Cutlers' Company on a site in Church Street adjoining the Cutlers' Hall, the predecessor of the present building, for £25 14s a year[73], say £2700 today (2008). Nevertheless the Spurrs were not too hard up to pay for their daughter's education.

Baptised on 14 September 1774 at St Peter's Church (which was to become Sheffield Cathedral in 1914), young Hannah was to attend a day school at the vicarage, Broom Hall, where the formidable James Wilkinson held sway.[74] Comments about her childhood range from the hagiographical to the down-to-earth. On the one hand she was 'the embodiment of amiability and benevolence', working her way down a nominal roll of poor people to relieve with her pocket money and at about the age of 10 regularly leaving her playmates to attend evening prayer.[75] On the other, she started to keep juxtaposed lists of her good and bad deeds, but when the bad ones outstripped the good she gave this up. When she was about 12 her mother died. Under the supervision of a non-resident married sister she took charge of her family for two years until her father's death, when they were dispersed. For another two years she was sent to a boarding school at Chesterfield, where she was rather too bright for the master's comfort.

Back in Sheffield, Hannah spent the rest of her teens torn between hedonism and spirituality.[76] About 1794 she became involved with the Methodists of Norfolk Street Chapel. Despite strong opposition by some of her family, she joined them in 1796,[77] when a great revival was in train under the ministry of William Bramwell. That same year, on 2 July, she wrote: 'This morning I have given myself to God'.[78] But Norfolk Street did not retain her much longer; she was among the lost gemstones commemorated by the Superintendent, James Wood, at the end of his short summary of membership – there is no detailed list – for 1797:

> In August, 1797, a dreadful division of the Sheffield Society was effected by artful men, and a loss in town and country sustained of about 1,200 members. Where will these be found when the Lord shall make up his jewels?[79]

For on 18 August Hannah had finally disregarded her friends' objections and attended Scotland Street Chapel, which Alexander had taken over from the ailing Methodist rebel Thomas Bryant. He had preached on Ps 91:4, 'His truth shall be thy shield and buckler', and Hannah, never prone to excitement, recorded: 'The presence of God was, I believe, generally felt in the meeting. My soul was calm and happy'.[80] Her reticence – and perhaps, as her stepdaughter thought, painful later memories – prevented her later from writing up an account of her courtship from her contemporary notes.[81] Some of their love-letters survived, however, revealing them as a couple of unequal warmth. Alexander called her 'my beloved Hannah', once averring that next to divine grace she was 'the choicest favour that earth could afford'. She replied with her blessing and gratitude – for what? – for his interest in the Sunday School! For their strongest bond was 'a mutual desire, not merely for each other's, but the general good'. They were married in Sheffield Parish Church on 12 April 1798, the witnesses including Peter and Sarah Spurr, Hannah's siblings, and Sally joined them from Epworth.[82] The sisters were close: many years later someone was to picture them together in the pew at a missionary meeting, both unassuming and plainly dressed.[83] Yet they were certainly not shrinking violets. Life would soon require Hannah in particular to show her strength of character.

Alexander, Hannah and Sally

Although we have no contemporary accounts of Hannah's and Sally's first meeting or early life together, comments by Sally (Sarah) in adulthood suggest that they bonded very quickly. She described Hannah as 'my precious mother' and 'my beloved mother', and herself as 'her daughter'.[84] The extended Epworth family encouraged this. Writing to Alexander on 21 May, mainly to oppose the principle and practice of a paid ministry ('hireling priests'), his brother Thomas added:

> You will desire Salley to give me a few lines to let me know how she goes on with her learning and whether she improves in writing or not and to be very diligent in business and to obey her mother in all things.[85]

It is then no surprise that later writers referred to Sarah as the daughter of Alexander and Hannah Kilham.[86]

As MNC secretary, on top of his considerable travelling, it fell to Alexander to bear the brunt of organizing the 1798 Conference. For the first time, his burden appeared to be too much for him, and the normally imperturbable Hannah became alarmed. They moved to his new station in Nottingham. The chapel was in Goosegate, Hockley, near the corner of Belward Street.[87] A health improvement turned out to be short-lived, and in September an uncharacteristic new note appeared in his writing: 'I am just harassed out of my life by preaching, travelling and want of rest'. He tried to rally – 'my mind is comfortable and happy' – but we are not convinced, and neither in fact was he: 'Rest seems desirable; but I must not have it in this world'.[88] Did he sense that he would soon have it in the next?

Hannah had no doubt that Alexander's 'uncommon exertions' hastened his death. In the autumn he made a preaching tour to rainy Wales, accompanied by his wife and daughter as far as Merthyr Tydfil. He rode on to Brecon through frost and deep snow. Hannah, full of forebodings, wrote to him the next day with unusual feeling: 'I do not know that ever I found it so hard to part from you as yesterday'. She would pray for him every night at 6 o'clock. Then she made a comment about Sally which in the light of later events is revealing not only of the little girl's intellectual ability but also of her stepmother's perspicacity: 'Our dear Child is well. I have observed toda[y with] satisfaction that the powers of her mind are strong'.[89]

Alexander's physical strain was combined with mental stress when a critic resurrected the old charge that he had caused his first wife's death and added that he had done much to ruin her successor. He wrote once again to refute this ten days before he died. Hannah later recalled speaking to him on his deathbed about the great happiness he had given her, though for such a short time. She also remembered Sally saying to the servant two days before the end that 'she had never heard him pray so' (fervently?) before. Alexander asked Hannah to safeguard for Sally the inheritance from his first wife, and she promised to bring his dear child with her to heaven; 'I told him my heart was fast bound to hers'.[90] Alexander died on 20 December 1798, aged 36, at the preachers' house in Hockley. He was interred in the chapel wall. Sally was barely 10 years old. Hannah was 24, married for eight months and eight days, and nearly six months pregnant.

She wrote to tell Alexander's mother-in-law Hannah Gray about his death and also to enquire about the allowance that he had irregularly sent to the old lady. The reply survives, addressed to 'My Dear Daughter', with condolences, thanks and several references to Sally: '...be pleased to let me know if my Dear child is to continue with you... my family is exceeding well satisfied that dear little Salley is with such a mother as they are exceeding anxious of her welfare and yours also'. She ended by inviting them to visit in the summer.[91] The letter does not convey the same sense of urgency as the one to Alexander following her daughter's death, and she was no doubt grateful for young Hannah's commitment to the little girl.

Epworth Again and New Directions

Hannah's own daughter and only child, Mary, was born on 3 April 1799. Then, according to her stepdaughter, she 'took charge of the female part of a Methodist day school' in Nottingham.[92] This seemingly straightforward statement is problematic. In 1796 the 'Methodist School' in Nottingham had probably over 700 pupils and six years later nearly 900.[93] The effect of the schism of 1797 was that management passed to the MNC but Wesleyan adherents went on giving their services.[94] It was, however, a Sunday school, and S.D. Chapman states categorically that no day schools were established between the High Pavement charity school of 1788 (the third such foundation) and the Lancasterian Boys' School of 1810.[95]

It is of interest that eighteen months earlier the educationist William Singleton had written to Alexander Kilham from Nottingham with very detailed ideas about Sunday schools there, and a recommendation of Miss Spurr, whom he later called 'my dear friend', for a teaching post. She procrastinated, doubtless because of her developing relationship with Alexander in Sheffield. Indeed when sending 'best respects to Miss S & y^r self' in January 1798 William evidently regarded them as an item.[96] So the basis had been laid for Hannah to take on this work. Certainly arithmetic was being taught to boys and sewing to girls on two or three evenings a week, in a reaction to teaching such subjects on Sundays, at a new MNC school of 1804,[97] but as we shall see, this could not have involved Hannah. That she herself had got it wrong when later reminiscing to her step-daughter would be surprising. In the light of a letter written to an acquaintance the day after Mary's birth, it would also be unlikely:

> Our friends in this place are engaged in forming a day-school, on a plan designed to promote the cultivation of religious principles. A committee of our friends are conducting the business relative to the formation of the school; but we shall be able to give a more perfect account of this, I hope, shortly.[98]

If the scheme had fallen through, Sarah would hardly have been led to present it as a fact.

In June 1800 Hannah took Sally and Mary to stay with her father-in-law at Epworth. He was in his early 70s now and ailing after a stroke. The younger Simon had assumed his father's various mantles, including charge of the sacking business and hospitality to the preachers. When in 1803 the New Connexion finally had to quit the old chapel and met first in an old barn and then in Simon Kilham's house,[99] this must have been either with the younger Simon's blessing or in his own house, since the older Simon had died early in the previous year. In 1803-04 the first MNC chapel at Epworth, Providence in Church Street, was built and opened, on land given by Simon the younger who had also helped considerably with the costs.[100] He is described as a taciturn man, a 'practical Christian' if not very energetic.[101] Should this last trait be reckoned a shortcoming, his minister and obituarist certainly thought it outweighed by his qualities: 'A man of peace... the most unassuming of Christian men... never envious... a loving husband, a kind parent... a sincere friend; open and generous in his disposition, and easy of access... an excellent leader and much beloved by the members of his [chapel] class'.[102] As Sally wrote to him occasionally in adulthood, and no correspondence with her other uncles survives, we may hazard a guess that he was her favourite.

The middle uncle, Richard, remains the most shadowy, but along with one of the Simons he was among the five pro-MNC trustees of the shared chapel.[103] He had a numerous family – eight children appear in the parish registers of baptisms – and early in the new century is believed to have taken on a farm on the north-western outskirts of Epworth; the former farmhouse is now known as Croft Ends.[104] Thomas, Sally's youngest uncle, clock and watchmaker, comes across from correspondence as humourless and opinionated, not above lecturing his eminent brother. Old Simon once wrote to Alexander that Thomas 'has begun to preach & some like to hear him'.[105] This was scarcely a ringing endorsement. Yet he seems to have been a conscientious worker for the cause. A minister recorded with appreciation how he had accompanied him round the village making a house-to-house collection for the chapel. Thomas also lived out his faith: the same witness testified that when a probationary minister, Benjamin Blagborough, was severely disabled in a coach accident, he took him into his home, taught him the skill of clock-making and helped him to open a small shop in Thorne.[106] A Sunday school where local tradesmen learned to read and write was held in Thomas's shop.[107] He was married but no record of children has been found.

The summer 1800 visit to Epworth marked a critical point in Hannah Kilham's life and, through her influence, in Sally's too. For several months Hannah had been feeling dissatisfied with her spiritual life and with her experience of Methodism. It sounds from her memoirs as if the constant stress of her husband's last year – followed surely by the strain of coping with widowhood – had left her longing for harmony and peace, both in her own mind and in the life of the Church. She continued to value the compassionate tradition in Methodism, but otherwise found it wanting.

It is unclear where Hannah had her first contact with Quakers, but if it was in 1799 or early 1800 it must have been in Nottingham. She confided to her journal:

> If ever I express a wish to join them it will be because I believe them to be the most faithful, as well as the most enlightened, people I know of, and that I am called of God to spend my days among them.[108]

The word 'enlightened' evokes the cardinal Quaker principle of the Light within men and women – ever since George Fox had written 'I was commanded to turn people to that inward light' – the illumination of thought and feeling breaking into their consciousness, transforming their nature and leading them on, experienced particularly in the meeting.[109] Uncharacteristically restless, Hannah went to the Quaker meeting at Epworth and had something of an ecstatic experience. Back in her room, reflecting on John 3:17, she recorded: 'The words sank into my soul: a light shone on them, of such as I had never before been sensible'.[110] The Christian context of her future life and ministry was to be the Society of Friends, as it was for many years to be Sally's. According to one account she was following the example of her sister Sarah Spurr,[111] but it was not until May of that year that the latter joined the Friends, in Liverpool.[112]

Returning to Nottingham, on 18 August 1800 Hannah wrote to the class-leaders' meeting of Hockley Chapel to resign her office. She gave her reasons: she disapproved of the established ministry, of complaisant rather than challenging preaching, and of singing and praying because it was customary rather than sincere and spontaneous. She was also critical of her own past insincerity,[113] which should not surprise us as self-criticism used to be as conventional among keen Protestants as confession among Catholics. All this did not mean, however, that the Quakers had in her view attained perfection. Moving back to Sheffield a year later, she would attend their meetings but was in no rush to join them.[114] In any case they had their probationary procedures. It was not until early 1803 that Balby Monthly Meeting – the district executive of local Preparative Meetings in South Yorkshire – received and shortly afterwards granted her application for membership.[115]

Hannah had come back with the two children to Sheffield perhaps because the atmosphere in Nottingham was now strained and perhaps because she had been offered work there. In any event, she took up teaching in a day school run by a friend.[116] Tragedy struck again in January 1802 when her little daughter Mary fell victim to a scarlet fever epidemic and died.[117] Sally, 13, was now her last close link with Alexander – as we saw, her kindly father-in-law Simon Kilham also died about this time – but though they were to regard each other as mother and daughter, according to Dickson outward expressions of affection were made very difficult for Hannah by this final blow.[118] A bond of love had formed, never to be broken, but it had an abstract quality that would help to inure Sarah later to physical separation and independence.

Notes and References

[1] 'Connexion', always with an 'x', was a technical term not confined to the MNC, meaning a body of interdependent parts. Within Methodism it was later replaced by 'Church'. In 1907 the MNC became a component of the United Methodist Church which itself came together with the Wesleyans and the Primitive Methodists in 1932 to form the Methodist Church. The United Methodist Church of the USA dates from a 1968 merger and is a quite different entity.

[2] The Epworth parish registers have been transcribed and published in a series of booklets by the Isle of Axholme Family History Society. A Richard Kilham was buried on 24 Feb 1826 aged 62 but the dates do not quite fit. Thomas was baptised on 15 Feb 1765 and buried 19 Oct 1826 aged 62.

[3] 'An Account of Simon Kilham. By his Son', *The Methodist [MNC] Magazine, or Evangelical Repository* (hereafter *MMER*), 5 (1802), pp 185-6. The author is probably Simon junior, the most prominent of the three Kilham sons remaining in Epworth.

[4] J. Wesley, *Journal*, 3 (London, 1915, 1938), p 19.

[5] 'An Account', pp 186-7.

[6] Ibid., p 378. See also Wesley's testimony in the *Journal*, 6 (1938), pp 351-3. His editor, N. Curnock, is less than clear about the two Simons, but this edition offers more on the Epworth background (here and p 520) than the later one, *The Works of John Wesley, 23: Journal and Diaries VI (1776-86)*, ed. W.R. Ward and R.P. Heitzenrater (Nashville, TN, 1995), pp 239-40, 319.

7 Wesley, 6, pp 351-3.
8 'An Account', p 379.
9 anon. [J. Blackwell], *Life of the Rev. Alexander Kilham* (London and Manchester, 1838), pp 52-6, gives a full picture of his protracted coming to faith. Henceforth cited as Blackwell.
10 Ibid., p 62.
11 'An Account', pp 378-9.
12 Blackwell, pp 103-7.
13 J. Grundell and R. Hall, ed., *The Life of Mr Alexander Kilham, Methodist Preacher...* [by himself], (Nottingham, 1799), pp 38-9. Blackwell (p 109) omits the account of their meeting. Kilham and Blackwell use the spelling 'Grey', her family 'Gray'.
14 A. Kilham, *A Short Account of the Life and Death of Mrs Sarah Kilham* (Leeds, 1797), p 5; North Yorkshire Record Office (NYRO), Northallerton: copy of Bishop's Transcripts, Pickering Marriages 1777-1812.
15 This is the purport of Blackwell, p 110.
16 Kilham, p 3; NYRO: copy of Bishop's Transcripts, Pickering Baptisms 1747-1792.
17 NYRO: copy of Bishop's Transcripts, Pickering Marriages 1696-1757.
18 Kilham, p 4; John Rylands University Library of Manchester, Methodist Archives Research Centre (MARC): Hobill Collection, Sheffield Deposit, Box 324 (2), Hannah Gray to AK, 7 Mar 1797. References hereafter to Methodist Church archives begin with MARC and go on to the box number or other reference. With regard to their correspondence the various Kilhams are cited thus: AK, Alexander; HK, Hannah; SiK, Simon senior; SK, Sarah junior (later SB, Sarah Biller); SK(S), Sarah senior; TK, Thomas.
19 NYRO: PR/PI22, Pickering Burials Register 1700-1812.
20 Kilham, p 3.
21 Ibid., p 4.
22 NYRO: copy of Bishop's Transcripts, Pickering Marriages 1754-1777; G. Home, *The Evolution of an English Town* (London, 1905), p 292.
23 NYRO: R/M/PI I 1/3/1-2, Methodist membership lists, Pickering, 1777-1812 (unless it was another Hannah Gray).
24 Blackwell, pp 108-9.
25 Grundell and Hall, ed., p 43.
26 C. Ellis, *St Peter & St Paul Parish Church, Pickering* (Derby, 2004), pp 3-5, 16.
27 Blackwell, p 122. Kilham won; there is no Anglican baptismal record. His attitude to the Church of England is traceable to an incident back in the Grimsby Circuit. Blackwell (pp 73-7) shows how the incumbent of Skendleby, near Spilsby – ironically, Squire Brackenbury's brother – forced him to declare himself a dissenter under the Toleration Act in order to continue preaching.
28 Kilham, p 7; Blackwell, p 147.
29 The Editor [B. Gregory], 'Alexander Kilham', *Wesleyan Methodist Magazine* (hereafter *WMM*), 6th Series, 11 (1887), p 692.
30 E.A. Rose puts 'banished' in quotation marks in his article 'Kilham, Alexander' in J.A. Vickers, ed., *A Dictionary of Methodism in Britain and Ireland* (Peterborough, 2000), p 191. For a fuller analysis of Kilham's reformist cam-

paign against the Methodist leadership, see the same author's 'The Methodist New Connexion 1797-1907: Portrait of a Church', *Proceedings of the Wesley Historical Society* (hereafter *PWHS*), 47 (1990), pp 241-4.

31 F. Baker, 'Ordinations by Wesley's Preachers', *PWHS*, 24 (1944), p 102. The ordination certificate is dated 19 May 1792.

32 Kilham, pp 7-8; Blackwell, p 173.

33 MARC: MAM PLP 64.36.8, AK to J. Gaulter, 12 Nov 1792. 'R—' represents a name indecipherably superimposed on another.

34 H.R. Bowes, 'Alexander Kilham's Cash Book', *PWHS*, 50 (1996), p 184.

35 Kilham, pp 8-10; Blackwell, pp 179, 216-17.

36 Kilham, p 13.

37 Rose, 'Kilham, Alexander'.

38 MARC: Box 324 (2), under Eversfield, SK(S) to AK, 15 and 21 July 1796; Kilham, p 15; Grundell and Hall, ed., p 115.

39 Ibid.

40 MARC: Box 324 (2), S. Eversfield to AK, 30 July 1796.

41 MARC: Box 324 (4), SK(S) to AK, 3 Aug 1796. This was too much for Blackwell, who altered it to 'rejoicing at what they supposed to be our downfall' (p 257).

42 SK(S) to AK, 20 Aug 1796, cited in Rose, 'The Methodist New Connexion', p 243; E presumably stands for Eversfield.

43 Kilham, pp 16-20; Blackwell, pp 292-3, 303-7.

44 MARC: MAM PLP 64.36.7, AK to W. Franklin, 22 Nov 1796.

45 MARC: among correspondence in Box 324 (1).

46 Kilham, pp 18-22. The respective texts were Rev 14:13, 2 Sam 12:21-23 and Heb 9:27.

47 Information from E.A. Rose.

48 MARC: Box 324 (2), Thomas Gray to AK, 7 Mar 1797; spelling corrected.

49 NYRO: R/M/PI I 1/3/1-2.

50 MARC: Box 324 (2), Hannah Gray to AK, 7 Mar 1797.

51 Blackwell, p 196.

52 MARC: Box 324 (3), SiK to AK, 28 Feb 1797; spelling corrected.

53 Kilham, p 26; Blackwell, pp 216-17, 310-12.

54 Ibid., p 316.

55 Grundell and Hall, ed, pp 145-6.

56 Isle of Axholme Family History Society, Epworth Parish Registers transcripts.

57 Lincolnshire Archives: LQS, Land Tax, Manley 1795, 1800; Tonge 2/99.

58 MARC: Box 324 (3), SiK to AK, 9 May 1797.

59 L. Stone, *The Family, Sex and Marriage in England 1500-1800*, rev. edn (London, 1979, repr. 1990), p 260.

60 F. Baker, 'The Beginnings of Methodism in Lincolnshire', *Journal of the Lincolnshire Methodist Historical Society*, 4 (1988), no 1, p 10. He notes that W. Myles, *A Chronological History of the People called Methodists* (1813 edn), gives a 1758 date.

61 Rose, 'The Methodist New Connexion', pp 243-6.

62 'An Account', p 420 (Simon senior); C. Atkinson, 'Obituary: Mr Simon Kilham', *Methodist New Connexion Magazine and Evangelical Repository* (hereafter *MNCM*), 40 (1837), p 233 (Simon junior).

63 See the controversy between B. Gregory and J. Gibson in *WMM*, 6th Series, 11-12 (1887-88), starting at 11, p 689 and continuing intermittently to 12, p 551.

64 MARC: MAM PLP 64.36.4.

65 MARC: Box 324 (3), TK to AK, 27 Feb 1797 and SiK to AK, 21 Aug 1797; E.A. Rose, 'The First Methodist New Connexion Chapels', *PWHS*, 36 (1967), pp 11, 14; Rose, 'The Methodist New Connexion', p 244.

66 W. Seaton, 'Methodism in the Thorne Circuit', *MNCM*, 36 (1833), p 279.

67 Blackwell, p 50; G. Wall, 'Reminiscences of the Kilham Family', *MNCM*, 52 (1849), p 126.

68 Rose, 'The Methodist New Connexion', p 244: 'A part of the Sheffield society and circuit'.

69 S. Biller, ed., *Memoir of the Late Hannah Kilham, Chiefly Compiled from her Journal* (London, 1837), p 24.

70 T. Davies, 'Photos of Eminent Females: Mrs Alexander Kilham', *MNCM*, 89 (1886), p 83. Unfortunately the 'photos' are purely verbal.

71 R.E. Leader, *History of the Company of Cutlers in Hallamshire*, 2 (Sheffield, 1906), p 355.

72 Biller, ed., p 1.

73 Leader, 1 (1905), p 189.

74 M. Dickson, *The Powerful Bond: Hannah Kilham 1774-1832* (London, 1980), p 15.

75 Davies, pp 83-4.

76 Biller, ed., pp 1-3, 478; Dickson, p 16.

77 Biller, ed., p 479; Sheffield Archives (SA): NR 349, Sheffield Methodist Circuit, Roll of Members 1792-1807, 'An Account of Sheffield Circuit 1796'. She could not have 'officially joined' in 1794 (Dickson, p 21, misinterpreting an imprecise comment by Biller); no other Hannah Spurr figures, and she herself appears at no other date.

78 Biller, ed., p 4.

79 SA: NR 349, referring to Mal 3:17.

80 Biller, ed., p 26.

81 Ibid., p 29.

82 Ibid., pp 42-3, 46; SA: PR 138/106 (marriage register).

83 J. Holland and J. Everett, *Memoirs of the Life and Writings of James Montgomery*, 5 (London, 1856), p 157.

84 Biller, ed., pp i, 59, 128, 365.

85 MARC: Box 324 (3), TK to AK, 21 May 1798; spelling corrected.

86 J. Benson, *Quaker Pioneers in Russia* (London, 1902), p 94; editorial comment by R.E. Leader in T.A. Ward, *Peeps into the Past* (London and Sheffield, 1909), p 196, possibly based on Benson.

87 For a brief history, see R.C. Swift, 'Hockley Chapel, Nottingham', *PWHS*, 42 (1980), p 123.

88 Blackwell, pp 369, 379-80.

89 Ibid., pp 381-2; MARC: Box 324 (3), HK to AK, 5 Nov 1798 (text in brackets missing and conjectured); 'Extract of a Letter from Mrs Kilham to Mrs Heaps', *MMER*, 2 (1799), p 331.

90 Biller, ed., pp 54, 59; Blackwell, pp 384, 386-92.

91 MARC: Box 324 (2), Hannah Gray to HK, 27 Jan 1799.
92 Biller, ed., p 60.
93 S.D. Chapman, 'The Evangelical Revival and Education in Nottingham',
    Transactions of the Thoroton Society of Nottinghamshire, 66 (1962), p 37. For
    the history of the school see also R.C. Swift, 'Methodist Sunday Schools in
    Nottingham', *PWHS*, 33 (1961), pp 17-20, 36-40.
94 Ibid., p 36.
95 Chapman, p 48. He calls the High Pavement school Presbyterian; cp. J.
    Blackner, *The History of Nottingham* (Nottingham, 1815), p 126, and W.H.
    Wylie, *Old and New Nottingham* (London, 1853), p 342, where it is desig-
    nated Unitarian.
96 MARC: Box 324 (4), William Singleton to AK, 25 Oct 1797, 4 Jan 1798 and
    (for 'my dear friend') 25 May 1798. Dickson (p 62) is wrong in associating
    the start of Hannah's and Singleton's acquaintanceship with events of 1803.
97 Blackner, p 128.
98 'Extract of a Letter', pp 332-3.
99 Seaton, p 279; Rose, 'The First Methodist', p 14.
100 Wall, p 126.
101 Ibid.; Atkinson, p 233.
102 Ibid., p 234.
103 MARC: Box 324 (3), SiK to AK, 9 May 1797.
104 Information from Stanley Johnson.
105 MARC: Box 324 (3), SiK to AK, 28 Feb 1797; TK to AK, 27 Feb and espe-
    cially 21 May 1798.
106 Wall, pp 126-7.
107 C. Ella, *Historic Epworth* (Oxford, 1994), p 57.
108 Biller, ed., pp 65, 72-3; quotation p 74.
109 J. Sykes, *The Quakers* (London, 1958), pp 28-31.
110 Biller, ed., p 76.
111 Holland and Everett, 5, note to p 157.
112 Manchester Central Library (MCL): M85/1/4, entries for 28 Apr and 26 May
    1803.
113 Biller, ed., pp 77-8; Dickson, p 60 (q.v., pp 52-62, for a full account of
    Hannah's 'spiritual struggles'); A. Twells, '"Let us begin well at home": Class,
    Ethnicity and Christian Motherhood in the Writing of Hannah Kilham, 1774-
    1832', in E.J. Yeo, ed., *Radical Femininity* (Manchester, 1998), pp 31-2.
114 J.O. Greenwood, *Quaker Encounters, 1: Friends and Relief* (York, 1975), note
    to p 115, asserts that Hannah Kilham and Sarah came from the '"Independent
    Methodists" (often called "Quaker Methodists" because they shared some
    Quaker views and allowed the ministry of women)'. He gives no evidence for
    a literal understanding of this statement, nor have we found any. The Quaker
    Methodists were active in Warrington from 1796 to 1806 when they joined
    the new union of Independent Methodists, retaining their local name for
    many years (J.A. Dolan, 'An Independent Methodist Bicentenary', *PWHS*,
    50 (1996), pp 237-9). Although Hannah may have come across them during
    her brief stay in Liverpool, eighteen miles away, in 1803 or 1804 (see the next
    chapter), she had committed herself to the Society of Friends early in 1803.

Perhaps, however, Greenwood merely meant that she was a Quaker with a Methodist background and certain Methodist traits.

[115] Biller, ed, p 90. The original minutes for this year are missing. Balby (now in Doncaster) was the initial setting, but the rotation of meetings at this time comprised Doncaster, Sheffield and Thorne. By a strange coincidence, the original small group at Balby in the 1650s included brothers John and Thomas Killam. George Fox reputedly preached in the orchard at John's farm. John, his wife Margaret and Thomas joined Fox as travelling preachers (R. Hoare, *Balby Beginnings: The Launching of Quakerism* (Sheffield, 2002), especially pp 27-8, 47, 111). I have read somewhere that Alexander Kilham had Quaker ancestors.

[116] Biller, ed., p 87; no details available.

[117] She died on 18 January (SA: QR 67, Births, Marriages and Deaths 1691-1909 [miscellaneous transcripts]).

[118] Dickson, pp 60-1.

2. BRITISH SCHOOLS AND
RUSSIAN PROJECTS

SARAH'S SHEFFIELD YEARS

Schools and Societies

SALLY NOW becomes Sarah. She is a teenager, and we do not meet the childhood name again. For the next two decades – apart from a possible interlude about 1803-04 when Hannah Kilham and her sister Sarah Spurr were temporarily teaching at the Friends' School in Liverpool[1] – she would be engrossed through and alongside her stepmother in three associated activities in Sheffield: education, Quakerism and good works. Before looking at these, however, let us too make a quick visit across the Pennines. Frustratingly, the relevant archives of the Liverpool Quakers were destroyed by fire, so the Liverpool piece of the jigsaw of Hannah's life seems to be lost.[2] Yet records of the Manchester Friends' School do survive. We shall use them to get a rough idea of the Liverpool undertaking. (We assume here that our source about Hannah and her sister was accurate, and that such a school really existed; but even if it did not, the Manchester experience has its own fascination.)

In 1795 Manchester Friends decided to set up a school 'for the religious Education of their Children', managed by a committee under the Preparative Meeting and financed from subscriptions and fees. The committee was to provide teachers, admit and 'dismiss' children, superintend the school and fix the fees.[3] Reading English cost 5s per quarter, all 3 Rs 7s 6d, and 'Instruction in the Languages' 12s.[4] (The fee for the 3 Rs alone would come to about £30 a quarter in 2008 money.)[5] Children who did not belong to Manchester Preparative Meeting were not excluded but their parents had to pay double. Religious instruction was not mentioned but attendance at 4th Day Meeting (on Wednesdays) was compulsory.[6] By 1802, when Hannah's future brother-in-law Matthew Corbett was both a member of the committee and a 'school visitor', there were 31 pupils, all of whom were learning English, 25 writing and arithmetic, 12 Latin, 6 French and 2 Greek. Those only learning to read English, it appears, attended half-time. The school was open to both boys and girls but the latter were a small minority.[7]

The original nine School Rules make interesting reading. Hours were from 9 to 12 and 2 to 5. Otherwise they are nearly all about behaviour: arriving with clean hands and faces and refraining from unnecessary talking in school, untruths, gossip, quarrelling, sticks and stones, striking and teasing one another, complaining about trifles and gambling. Buying, receiving and exchanging from each other required permission. Although these rules reflect Quaker sobriety, we can imagine them laid down in any school where moral values were emphasized. Yet two others leave us in no doubt that we are in a Quaker school. One is about plainness of speech: 'That they make use of the words thou and thee, when speaking or writing to a single Person, and call the days of the week and the months of the Year numerically as first, second, third &c'. The other warns boys not to pull off their hats and girls not to curtsey; such conduct, it is asserted, is contrary to Scripture.[8] Thus signs of Quaker distinctiveness are numbered among moral principles, like rituals identifying the group and reinforcing its sense of identity.

In 1806, with her colleague Elizabeth Albiston, Hannah Kilham set up her own day school in Sheffield, occupying part of the so-called Lord's

The Lord's House.

House on the north-east corner of Fargate and Norfolk Row.[9] The Lord here was not the Lord of the Church but the Lord of the Manor of Sheffield, the Duke of Norfolk. In 1706 Thomas Howard, the 8th Duke, had abandoned his local Tudor residence, the Manor Lodge, out in its park, and had replaced it with this modest town house as a base for his agent and for himself on his visits.[10] The Howards were Roman Catholics and the Lord's House also served as a meeting place for the Catholics of Sheffield. It was just along the road from the future site of the Catholic chapel of 1815 and St Marie's Church of the early 1850s, now St Marie's Cathedral.

The first advertisement of the school, in July, is not very informative, so below we reproduce the second which shows it to be up and running.[11] It also details the fees. For the 3 Rs, plus needlework, these are more than double those of its Manchester contemporary, but as yet it offers no expensive frills like foreign languages. The date-style reveals it as Quaker-run, but it is privately owned. It is not beholden to Sheffield Meeting, but probably plays a similar role to that of Manchester Friends' School with respect to the daughters of Sheffield Friends who could afford it and did not – or not yet – want to send them to the Friends' School at Ackworth.

DAY SCHOOL

H. KILHAM AND E. ALBISTON respectfully acknowledge the kindness of the Parents by whom Children have been entrusted to their care, and inform them and the Public that their School in Norfolk Row will be opened after the Winter Vacation on the 5th of 1st Month 1807.

TERMS

	L	S	D	
English Grammar, Reading and Needlework	0	12	6	Per Qr
Writing and Arithmetic	0	3	6	Addl.
Geography	0	5	0	Do.

Sheffield, 29th of 12th Month, 1806

Quaker sources mention the help of Sarah (at 17 clearly old enough to be useful) and Hannah's Mancunian niece Ann Corbett in founding and running the school.[12] 'Niece' is an honorary title: Ann was Matthew Corbett's eldest daughter from his first marriage, whereas Hannah's sister Sarah Spurr was his third wife, whom he married in 1805.[13] Ann had been a pupil at Ackworth in 1802-03,[14] and was slightly younger than Sarah Kilham. Sarah, by the way, nowhere mentions her own education. We must assume that she acquired part if not all of it from her mother and stepmother.

On the first few years of Mrs Kilham's school no other information is to be had, except that her address was still Norfolk Row in 1809.[15] Soon after this, however, there is clear evidence that it has established itself as a respectable and sought-after Quaker institution. An undated prospectus, which someone has tentatively dated to 1811, is complemented by a detailed advertisement (see below).[16] By then the school had developed a boarding side and moved out of the town to salubrious Western Bank, now the location of Sheffield University, then on the verge of becoming a smart new residential suburb. The advertisement differs from the prospectus, which alludes to the pupils' 'improvement… in Christian principles', in that from the double meaning of 'Friends' and again the date style it clearly shows Western Bank to be a Quaker school.

WESTERN BANK SCHOOL

HANNAH KILHAM respectfully acknowledges the kindness and liberality with which her School has been supported, and informs her Friends that her Vacation this summer will close on the 18th of 7th Month.

TERMS: BOARD AND INSTRUCTION, (Washing &c. included) THIRTY GUINEAS PER ANNUM. Weekly Boarders, Twenty-five Guineas per Annum.

	£	s	d
TO DAY SCHOLARS:			
Reading, Writing, Arithmetic, Needlework, English Grammar, Geography, Map-drawing (Writing Books, Pens and Reading Books included) per Quarter	0	18	0
Reading, Writing on Slates and other Instruction Suited to the youngest class, per Quarter	0	12	6

Dining with Hannah Kilham's Family, a Guinea and a Half per Quarter.
The French Language on the usual Terms.
Western Bank, near Sheffield, 6th Month, 20th, 1812.

Hannah displays a flexible admissions policy, catering as she does for full, weekly and day boarders as well as day scholars. Pupil numbers are not recorded but as dining was with the family the boarding side at least must have been modest, and a former pupil, Mary Howitt, describes the group marching to Sunday meeting as 'the little party'.[17] A downhill walk of just under a mile brings us from Western Bank to Hartshead, where Mary cherished the vain hope of glimpsing her hero James Montgomery, radical editor of the *Iris* newspaper, at work in his office,[18] but on Sunday mornings it was Queen Street Chapel that claimed him. Meetinghouse Lane still survives, though successive buildings familiar to Hannah, Sarah and the children do not. In the same year as the boarding school opened, the meeting house of 1764 was much extended and the old part retained as a room for women's meetings. Friends gathered in this rebuilt meeting house until 1940 when it fell a victim to bombs.[19]

We are given a full picture of the curriculum. It reflects to some degree Lawrence Stone's account of the upper middle class's (and gentry's) broadened expectations of education for their daughters around 1800: no longer the heavy stress on the social graces, but a range of subjects from the academic to the practical, to equip young women to be efficient and well-informed wives and mothers and companionable – though still subordinate – partners.[20] So here we find not only the three Rs but also

English grammar and geography. Among languages, the classical ones were left to boys' schools. (Did any of those Manchester girls break the mould?) Only French occurs as an apparent concession to gentility. Yet there are differences, which we may attribute to the serious-minded Quaker approach to schooling. We find no mention of deportment, music or dancing (which in most up-to-date girls' schools had been somewhat relegated but certainly not ousted altogether). Needlework remains, doubtless for utilitarian rather than social reasons, and it is interesting that the only kind of drawing is specifically *map* drawing. Literature is absent, presumably because it too was regarded as frivolous, as is history. Quite possibly, however, the small size of the school and its staff affected the range of subjects provided. Religion, it appears, was left to be caught, while its practical application in the form of social concern, as we shall shortly see, was taught by Hannah herself in a startlingly hands-on way.

'Dining with Hannah Kilham's family', an optional extra for day pupils, gives an impression of the intimacy of a small school. This is reinforced by a somewhat unexpected image of Hannah as a kindly tutor rather than a stern principal. To Frances Thompson, whose 11-year-old daughter was at the school in 1819, she wrote in evident haste:

> Mary had begun to write a letter this afternoon but having only essayed on the slate an account of arrival & written but a part of it when Mr and Mrs Hodgson arrived & wishing for her company in the garden I engaged to send the information for her.

She ended with the news that Mary had taken a walk to Endcliffe,[21] which many university students still do because they live there.

The curriculum was similar to that of the parallel boys' school. This, interestingly, had been opened at nearby Broomhall in February 1812 by Hannah's old friend and Methodist-turned-Quaker William Singleton, who in the meantime had been teaching at Ackworth.[22] In place of compulsory needlework the boys could take Latin as an extra, and at a guinea per quarter dayboys' fees were slightly higher than daygirls'. Dickson makes a significant comparison with the boarding fees at Ackworth (eight guineas a year);[23] whereas Ackworth's original remit was to cater for the children of Friends 'not in affluence', the Sheffield schools were nearly four times more expensive. Thirty guineas then would be more like £1500 in 2008, considering what such a sum might buy.[24] Although the full quarterly fees for day pupils were now 3s lower than in 1806, the youngest ones nevertheless paid about four times as much as pupils without free places at a country charity school some four miles distant just a few years later.[25]

Western Bank School evidently appealed to a select and well-off clientele, drawn from far beyond Sheffield. Mary Howitt confirms this: it was 'a Friends' school held in high repute'.[26] Among those who responded to the appeal were the Thompsons of Liverpool, whose daughter Mary we recently met. Thomas Thompson had studied pharmaceutical chemistry under William Allen (1770-1843), head of the firm of manufacturing chemists which would later be famous as Allen & Hanburys, a leading Quaker philanthropist and a defining influence on the career of Sarah Kilham. Thomas married Frances Phillips, the sister of two eminent scientist brothers whom he had met at William Allen's. The Thompsons moved to Liverpool where he too established a business as a pharmaceutical and manufacturing chemist. The firm prospered. Later a Quaker minister, Thomas became well known as an antiquarian and collector in scientific fields and Frances shared his interests.[27] She was also a friend of Hannah Kilham and thus of Sarah, who kept up the link after her stepmother's final departure for Africa.

Another student was Candia Barrow,[28] daughter of an overseas merchant and shipowner of Lancaster. In 1832 she was to become the second wife of John Cadbury of Birmingham. He had set up as a tea and coffee dealer – selling cocoa nibs (broken roasted beans) as a sideline – in 1824 and graduated to cocoa and chocolate manufacturing in 1831.[29] Two of their sons, Richard and George, continued the dynasty.

Mary Howitt paints an interesting though perhaps disconcerting picture of certain extracurricular activities at the school:

> Hannah Kilham, an ever-helpful benefactress to the poor, devoted herself to a life of active Christian charity. She treated me as one of the older girls, I being tall for twelve, and often took me with her in her rounds. Once she sent me alone to a woman whose destitute condition so awoke my compassion as to induce me to bestow on her my last sixpence, with the hope uttered 'May the Lord bless it!' This was followed by self-questionings whether by my speech I had meant in my heart that the Lord should bless the gift to the sufferer or to me – then penniless.[30]

As Mary recalls it, the size of her sacrifice seems to eclipse the situation in which it was made. Yet this example of Hannah's upbringing methods causes us at least to raise our eyebrows.

On a different occasion, however, the school principal's behaviour appears bizarre even to the grown-up Mary and downright irresponsible to the modern reader:

> Another time at nightfall, Hannah Kilham made me wait in a desolate region of broken-up ground and half-built, ruinous houses while she visited some haunt of squalor. It seems strange that a highly conscientious woman should leave a young girl alone, even for a few minutes, in a low, disreputable suburb of a large town.

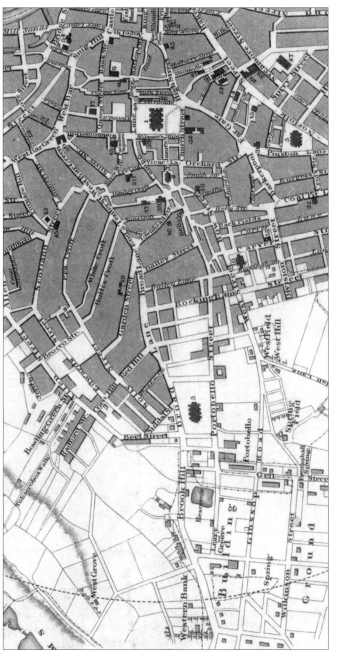

Leather's Plan of Sheffield in 1823 (detail). Scale: 9.3 cm to 1 km (6 in to 1 mile). Prominent at No1 is the Parish Church. To its NW is Scotland St Chapel (13). Close to its NE is the Friends Meeting House (8). Immediately to its S is Church St, where the original Spur cutlery works adjoined the Cutlers Hall (32). Further S is the site of Hannah Kilham's first school (Far Gate–Norfolk Row), near the Catholic Chapel of 1815 (14). On the W edge are the later school sites Western Bank and Leavy Greave. The school was last based in the northern third of the short terrace facing 'Leavy Greave' (now Leavy Greave Road).

But she was on what she felt to be her Master's errand, and I doubt
not had committed to His keeping; for whilst I was appalled by the
darkness and desolation around me, I saw the great comet of 1811
majestically careering through the heavens, and received an impression of Divine omnipotence which no school teaching could have
given me.[31]

In the end Mary chooses to accentuate the positive in her memory.
Contemporary parents clearly had a lot of faith in Hannah, undiminished
when news of such events filtered back. Two centuries later they would
have withdrawn their daughters from the school, though in our age of
heightened sensitivity about child protection a situation of this kind
becomes mere fantasy.

What was Sarah's role at the school? It was she who taught French.[32]
Hannah herself, writing to Frances Thompson, gives us a glimpse of the
young woman's domestic duties, meeting coaches and keeping a tally of
footwear:

The Shoe Bill is not a mistake – it is for three quarters of a year &
includes one pair of listing Shoes – SK has a book in which she
puts down every pair of shoes mended for each Girl separately &
every new pair – and checks the Bills with that book; she has looked
at both today & finds them right.[33]

Sarah and Ann Corbett were still on the staff in March 1819 when the
school re-opened in Leavy Greave.[34] Working back from successive census
returns, directories and town plans, we can pinpoint its location. There
were three large terraced houses in a street running north-south, a trace
of which remains in the short lane now called Leavy Greave Avenue, continuing Brunswick Street across Glossop Road. These houses faced east
down the hill still known as Leavy Greave Road. The northernmost one,
abutting on Western Bank where it became Brook Hill, was occupied by
the school. The modern pilgrim – or would-be instigator of a blue plaque
– will be somewhat confused by the more recent intrusion of Hounsfield
Road and Sheffield University's Hicks Building. The north-west end of
the Hicks Building and the grassy area between this and the Students'
Union is roughly where the school was. Sarah would have been pleased
and indeed amazed to know that the modest educational institution which
she helped to establish in this spot has been replaced by one extending
far and wide beyond it.

Hannah spent the following winter in London,[35] so either Sarah or
Ann or both of them must have been left in charge of the school. That
Sarah was prominent in its management is also suggested in a comment
by William Allen, who stated that *she* had been the one at the helm: 'she

kept a school and was doing exceedingly well'.[36] Given Hannah's many commitments, this was probably true in the spirit if not always in the letter.

Sarah had been accompanying her stepmother, and presumably the young boarders, to Meeting for Worship on Sunday mornings. On 9 July 1807 it was reported to Balby Monthly Meeting at Thorne that the 18-year-old had applied for membership, 'she being of orderly conduct and having diligently attended our Religious Meetings for a long time'. They decided that two of the men together with representatives of the Women's Meeting should visit her and report back.[37] One of the women, as it happened, was Barbara Hoyland, the sister of Daniel Wheeler whom we shall meet shortly and who was to be Sarah's first contact in St Petersburg. A month later the deputation acknowledged Sarah to be a well-disposed young person and a serious candidate deserving of sympathy, but gently recommended a further trial period.[38] Her case stayed on the agenda and eventually on 11 August 1808, the interviewers believing her to be 'in a good measure convinced of the principles of our profession', it was agreed to receive her into membership.[39] In Friends' terminology, she, like Hannah, had become a Quaker 'by convincement'. Unlike her stepmother, however, who was active in Sheffield Meeting business from 1808 until at least 1811, visiting sick and unemployed members and determining help from the meeting's funds,[40] Sarah did not take on responsibilities among the Friends. She was possibly too young and probably too busy.

In a wider social context it was different. Hannah Kilham was involved in at least ten charitable societies at various times. As early as 1803 she took a leading part in forming the Sheffield Society for Bettering the Condition of the Poor, thus starting a long collaborative friendship with the newspaper editor-proprietor and poet James Montgomery,[41] idol of the young Mary Howitt. He had been brought up in the Moravian Church and attended Queen Street Congregational Chapel in Sheffield, but many of the activists in the Sheffield Bettering Society, as it was known for short, were Quakers.

Montgomery was to develop a lot of respect for Hannah. At a meeting with his friends he once described her as 'a truly conscientious and persevering woman'. But her perseverance was apt to make its mark on others: a Mrs Harwood who was also there said that whenever her sister and Mrs Kilham came to her house they invariably left her something to do for them. Montgomery commented, 'Yes; they form a capital pair of scissors for cutting out work'.[42] 'To cut out work' meant to prepare work for others to complete, like a tailor's cutter – or a teacher. Hannah was good at that.

Among the various lists printed in the Society's Report for 1809 are numerous surnames already, or soon to become, familiar to us. Hannah

Kilham was one of a committee of twelve 'Visitors', along with Jane Doncaster of Allen Street, a member of a leading Quaker dynasty in Sheffield (file-makers at this time). The six people whose duty it was to receive information on worthy candidates for assistance included Peter Spurr of Arundel Street, Hannah's cutler brother, who was not a Quaker, and Jarvis Brady of Townhead Cross, a grocer who was. Among some 170 subscribers, Peter Spurr was the second most generous at 4 guineas. 'Kilham, H. & daughter' (Sarah) subscribed 1½ guineas. One guinea was contributed by Jarvis Brady, Daniel Doncaster, James Montgomery and Daniel Wheeler, while William and Josiah Fairbank, land surveyors, each gave half a guinea.[43] The purchasing power of the guinea at this time was about £60 in 2008 terms.[44] Hannah remained an active supporter up to 1821.[45]

In 1807 Hannah Kilham joined James Montgomery and others in forming the Sheffield Society for Superseding the Necessity for Climbing Boys.[46] Other organizations claiming Hannah's support were the Society for Visiting and Relieving Aged Females (from 1810);[47] the Sheffield Bible Association (she attended its inaugural meeting, hosted by Quakers, on 26 November 1812);[48] a committee on the establishment of a school of industry for poor girls (1815), later the General Committee for the Girls' Lancasterian School of Industry;[49] the Church Missionary Society (from 1816), which helped her to develop educational links with West Africa;[50] the British and Irish Ladies' Society, set up to promote the welfare of Irish women and children (1822-23);[51] the British and Foreign School Society (BFSS), to which she subscribed from 1822 to 1827;[52] and around 1824 the Society for the Gradual Abolition of Slaves (sic).[53] On top of all this she was writing and publishing books and pamphlets on educational topics.

This list of the activities of the school principal – until the beginning of the 1820s, when radical change would occur – leads one to think that her deputies Ann Corbett and Sarah must have been kept extremely busy at their workplace. Nevertheless Sarah is known to have shared certain of Hannah's interests, not only as a subscriber to the Sheffield Bettering Society.[54] Her philanthropic concern for the poor had already chimed with her professional experience of education to lead her to join Hannah in promoting the Lancasterian School of Industry for Girls.[55] It was a combination which would soon exert a defining influence on her future life-path. So Joseph Lancaster, his system and its introduction into Sheffield merit a closer look.

Enter Joseph Lancaster

Joseph Lancaster (1778-1838), a sieve-maker's son, Quaker and teacher, set up his own school for boys in 1798. Its popularity and his inability to pay an assistant gave him the idea of using the older pupils to teach the younger ones, and this was the 'monitorial system' developed at his new school in the Borough Road, Southwark.[56] He seems to have lit on it independently of the Rev Andrew Bell, who had employed it in Madras in the 1790s, and indeed earlier pioneers have been found. Their two systems, applying the same principle in different ways, formed the organizational basis of institutions for the education of poor and working-class children promoted respectively by the Royal Lancasterian Society (1808, the future BFSS) and the National Society for the Education of the Poor in the Principles of the Established Church throughout England and Wales (1811, mercifully shortened to the National Society). While both British Schools (as Lancasterian Schools were later known) and National Schools were open to all, only in the former was religious teaching non-denominational. In the title of this chapter, by the way, the term 'British Schools' is deliberately ambiguous, covering not only Lancasterian schools in England and Russia but other schools in Britain (more precisely, England) associated with the Kilhams.

Between 1807 and 1810 Joseph Lancaster completed nineteen 'missionary journeys' in the cause of his system.[57] In February 1809 he was in Sheffield, giving a lecture which Hannah Kilham and James Montgomery attended. A speech, a public meeting, a committee, a subscription and a rented building later, a boys' school, fitted out under Lancaster's erratic direction, was opened with 320 pupils in Gibraltar Street on 5 June.[58] His energy had a dark side which sounds like manic depression. He got into debt and finally fell out with his leading sponsors in 1814.[59] The activist William Allen had met Lancaster in 1808 and become treasurer of the Royal Lancasterian Society. Six years later he attended the fateful general meeting in London on 21 May and wrote:

> ...the absolute separation from Lancaster was announced, and we took the title of 'The British and Foreign School Society'. Every thing went off admirably... the only damp upon our proceedings was our feeling for the poor infatuated man who first brought forward this beneficent system.[60]

Schools called Lancasterian continued to be set up.

Early in 1815 another public meeting was held in Sheffield in support of a proposed School of Industry for Girls, to be accommodated in the Methodist Sunday School at Red Hill, off Broad Lane. A committee of 36 ladies was formed, with the primary task of obtaining subscriptions and donations, and the list was headed by Mrs Kilham. By the next week Miss Kilham had helped to increase numbers to 45. By the autumn other premises adjoining the Boys' School in Gibraltar Street had been designated.[61] After the school was opened committee members acquired the additional role of 'visitors and superintendents'.[62] Sarah left the committee after two years but Hannah stayed on for a third, during which the ladies opened a preparatory or branch Lancasterian girls' school in a new MNC Sunday School building in Allen Street, next to the Gibraltar Street one.[63] In her journal she speaks of her enjoyment in giving a Scripture lesson to the youngest children.[64] She served again from 1820 to 1822.[65]

Two quotations from the summer of 1819 show the first faint breeze of the winds of change in the Kilhams' lives. In her letter to Frances Thompson, Hannah writes:

> ...do not say to me 'Where wilt thou leave thy own few sheep?' –
> *Little* children & *poor* people feel to me the proper objects for my
> care at present & not those alone who happen to be in my own
> native vale, but those of the same class in other places...[66]

Sarah might have made the same comment. More relevant to her, however, was a resolution passed at the 10th Anniversary Meeting of the Boys' Lancasterian School:

> That we hear with pleasure of the exertions which the magnani-
> mous Alexander of Russia is making to enlighten his vast empire,
> by establishing innumerable schools, on the plan of the British and
> Foreign School Society, and by most extensively encouraging the
> circulation of the Holy Scriptures.[67]

So how did these developments in faraway Russia come about, and how did news of them reach Sheffield?

Quakers and Russia

In early 19th-century Russia, in reaction to the French Revolution, anglophilia was strong among the nobility. After Napoleon's invasion of Russia in 1812 it spread to the intelligentsia. Meanwhile the imposing, charming but duplicitous Emperor, Alexander I (in power 1801-25), played the diplomatic game in accordance with changing circumstances while maintaining a cordial attitude towards eminent English visitors. The earlier half of his rule was by and large a liberal, reformist era. After 1812 he became more and more reactionary through the proxy of his favourite A.A. Arakcheev. Previously of a rakish reputation, he now sought solace in religion of a mystical kind. He liked to have audiences with spiritual advisers, not least Western Europeans. This is how Quakers first came into the story.

In 1813 the Russian Interior Ministry sent a young scientist, Joseph Hamel, to England on a fact-finding mission concerning industrial processes. He met Sir Humphrey Davy and through him William Allen. Allen interested Hamel so much in the monitorial system that the young man wrote a book on the 'method of mutual instruction' and presented it to the Emperor. In 1820 the Russian government paid for its publication.[68]

Alexander received the book readily because in the meantime he had become personally acquainted with its subject. He had made an official visit to England with the King of Prussia in the summer of 1814, attending

Alexander I in 1802, aged 25.

Quaker worship at the meeting house in St Martin's Lane, London. William Allen and two other Friends, Stephen (Étienne) Grellet and John Wilkinson, had an audience with him on 21 June and public education and the work of the BFSS were among the topics discussed.[69] The Emperor also visited the Borough Road School.[70] Allen followed this up through interviews and correspondence with Count Lieven, the Russian Ambassador, submitting an account of the system, with proposals for training Lancasterian teachers in England and for sending a person or persons to St Petersburg to help organize the first schools.[71] This resulted in November 1816 in the arrival of four young Russian trainee teachers at Borough Road to study Lancaster's system in theory and practice. They also experienced mutual instruction in a highly simplified personal way: a student teacher called James Heard taught them English and they taught him Russian. In 1819 after more educational studies in France, Switzerland and Germany they returned home to train teachers.[72]

A parallel development was the establishment in 1815 of a Lancasterian school by and for the Russian army of occupation in Maubeuge, near the future Belgian border in northern France; the method had recently been exported from Borough Road to Paris. Other army schools followed across the Empire. Meanwhile in 1817 James Heard, aged only 18, had been recruited by the Russian Chancellor, Count Rumyantsev, through the embassy secretary, Baron Shtrandman, to set up a Lancasterian school on the Count's estate at Gomel', now in south-eastern Belarus, returning to England in 1821.[73] The Count liked the school and built more. 'The Count's estate will become like a fruitful garden in the midst of a barren desert', wrote James.[74]

So the Lancasterian school movement began to spread in Russia, boosted by a visit by Grellet, in response to a missionary call there, and Allen, who after initial reluctance decided to join him. They arrived in St Petersburg on 12 November 1818 with an introduction to Prince Alexander Golitsyn, Minister of Religious Affairs and Public Education, with whom they established a rapport and through whom they received permission to visit schools and prisons – their main concerns – and hospitals. As well as these activities, Allen and Grellet were soon engaged in a cavalcade of contacts with members of the nobility and British expatriates. These included new friends such as John Venning (1776-1858) and his younger brother Walter (died 1821), wealthy bank representatives, who shared their interests and briefed them on recent developments. There were old ones like Dr John Paterson, who as an emissary of the British and Foreign Bible Society (BFBS) had joined his fellow Scot Robert Pinkerton in founding the St Petersburg (later Russian) Bible Society in 1813 and was now its principal organizer in the capital.[75] Founded in London in 1804, the BFBS was an interdenominational evangelical body dedicated to circulating the Scriptures 'without note or comment'.

Another old acquaintance was Daniel Wheeler (1771-1840). A Londoner, after being orphaned he had had a colourful career in the navy and army. He visited Sheffield to see his sister, Barbara Hoyland, at Woodhouse. Her husband was a Quaker and Daniel was introduced to the Friends at Woodhouse Meeting. He left the army and opened a seed shop in Sheffield at the top of High Street, also taking on a dealership in ale and porter, a dark beer. His vaults were actually beneath the Friends Meeting House. He became a member there in 1797, marrying Jane Brady of Thorne in 1800.[76] As 'Dealer in Porter', his entries as a father in the Quaker births register between 1801 and 1812 certainly stand out,[77] but it was a respectable trade. *The Methodist Magazine or Evangelical Repository* (New Connexion) of 1799 treated its readers to a lengthy recipe for brewing their own porter.[78] The temperance movement began only in the 1830s.

When Daniel's sixth child, Jane, was born in June 1816, he described himself as 'Farmer' at The Hills, near Sheffield.[79] Could this anonymous-sounding spot be the same as 'The Hill' (now Hill Farm), out in the wilds beyond Stannington to the north-west of the town, and a meeting-place for Quakers almost from their start?[80] It seems very likely.

Soon after this Daniel Wheeler responded to the Emperor's call for a volunteer to undertake large-scale land reclamation outside the capital. He made a preliminary visit in 1817, meeting Golitsyn and later Alexander, and came back to fetch his family. In summer 1818 they took up residence at Okhta, with 1000 acres of designated marshy land, a few miles from the centre of St Petersburg.[81] At this time the city had recently reached the place familiar to modern tourists as the Smolny, on the west bank of the River Neva just before its curve westwards towards the sea. Okhta was on the other side. There were further allocated lands to the south-west at Volkovo[82] and to the south at Shushary, a dozen miles out on the Moscow road. Daniel hosted the St Petersburg Quaker meetings which Allen and Grellet attended. He was soon to play a quite important part in the Kilham story.

One other member of Wheeler's party of 22 who had crossed the North Sea was the children's tutor, George Edmondson. He is the hero of a romantic tale. He had briefly been a pupil of William Singleton at Ackworth, where, presumably unbeknown to Singleton, at the age of 12 and at first sight he had fallen in love with his little daughter Ann. After Singleton left to found Broomhall School, George applied to be apprenticed to him and was accepted. Ann seems to have reciprocated George's feelings. Her parents eventually noticed how things were going and were unhappy about it. When Daniel Wheeler, who had sons at the school, asked Singleton for advice on getting a tutor, he recommended George, releasing him from his apprenticeship on condition that he did not correspond with Ann.[83]

George, now 19 and of an adventurous nature, made the most of his opportunity. Once in Russia he did not remain a tutor for long. A fellow resident at Broomhall had been a budding surveyor, William Fairbank – later a partner in the well-known Quaker firm flourishing in Sheffield from the mid-1730s to 1848[84] – who had infected the older trainee teacher with enthusiasm for his own future profession. When the promised Russian surveyor did not appear, George rose to the occasion so efficiently that the following summer he found himself in charge of reclamation of 50,000 acres at Volkovo. That his progress impressed the Singletons we can only conjecture, but it is a fact that after receiving one of William Singleton's letters Daniel Wheeler told him he was now free to correspond with Ann. Through the written word love blossomed, and George briefly returned home to marry her at the Sheffield Meeting House on 27 December 1821. After a few years in St Petersburg he feared for her health and they came back to England. Over half a century later their daughter Jane wrote a curious account of the lives of some of the Quakers of Yorkshire and St Petersburg and hinted that grandmother Singleton had been the real obstacle to the courtship.[85]

George Edmondson is important for our story because he was a voluminous correspondent. Many of his letters have been preserved and form the primary sources on the Wheeler project and related developments in St Petersburg. Most of the correspondence was addressed to his father or sister in Lancaster, but he also wrote to his old master and employer William Singleton, a conduit to Sheffield Meeting. A remarkable amount of other Quaker correspondence has survived, for example that of Daniel Wheeler and William Allen. News would have reached the Sheffield Friends through many strands in the network.

The year 1819 was an eventful one for elementary education. A group of masons – several of whom were also members of the Union of Welfare, a secret political society – organized a 'Free Society for the Establishment of Schools of Mutual Instruction' in St Petersburg, receiving imperial assent on 14 January. They opened their school for poor boys in a rented wooden building in the Kolomna quarter on 16 July, with 265 pupils by the following midsummer in eight classes based on graded levels of literacy.[86] It was conceived as a model school, and although it was the only one directly operated by the Free Society's Committee, that body helped to open and run many others and teachers were trained for naval, Polish and Finnish schools.[87]

Elementary schooling also continued a main concern for Allen and Grellet. On 14 February the two Quakers had an audience with the Emperor's mother, the Dowager Empress Maria Fyodorovna. She patronized various philanthropic educational institutions and in particular the Society for the Education of Girls of Noble Birth (the Smolny Institute, founded by her mother-in-law Catherine the Great in 1764 as the first ever girls' school in Russia), placed under her supervision by her husband Paul in 1796 along with its attached 'middle-class school'. Having toured such schools, Allen and Grellet expressed to her their concern about the lack of provision for girls of the poorer classes, which might do so much to improve the nation's social life. Allen told her about their work in England and she was clearly interested, wishing to keep a sketch he had made of a schoolroom on the Lancasterian plan.[88]

In February and March the Quakers had two cordial interviews with the Emperor. At the first meeting, as well as talking further about the school plan, they spoke about the 'Scriptural Readings' which they had been inspired to compile in horror-struck reaction to a primer containing 'impious and... very obscene sentiments' in use at a military Lancasterian school they had visited. He agreed to receive these through Golitsyn, Minister of Public Education. A few days later they learned that he had approved publication and ordered funding of 8000 roubles to be allocated for this purpose.[89]

At their final audience on 14 March, topics of discussion included the matter which they had raised with the Dowager Empress. Here is part of William Allen's account of that meeting:

> We put in a word for the poor girls, who are universally neglected here, that is, the very poorest class, and the Emperor said that his mother had told him what we had said to her upon this subject, that he certainly would attend to it, and that, yesterday, he had given orders for six schools for girls to be founded. He expressed his desire to have a school society established like the Bible Society, but earnestly wished that a member of our religious society, interested in this subject, as well as in that of prisons and the Bible cause, would come to reside in Petersburg for some time, saying that he would receive such a one with open arms. I had reason to understand what he meant, but my path is straight forward.[90]

Allen is saying here in code that he refused to rise personally to the imperial bait. So did Grellet. In fact they left St Petersburg two days later to continue their tour. We shall see later the extent to which Alexander's wish and command were fulfilled. The two projects which they represented seem to have been refined by Allen into one, forwarded to London and sent on the grapevine to Sheffield.

On 22 May Golitsyn set up a special 'Committee for the Establishment of Schools of Mutual Instruction' both to promote and to supervise them,[91] for the similarly titled Free Society had given rise to suspicion. Eighteen months later there were Lancasterian schools in some 20 cities of the Russian Empire, with 5400 pupils in 15 of the 20.[92] Apart from doubts about the military schools, fuelled by a regimental mutiny in October 1820, their future looked bright. Yet sooner or later the skies over most of them would darken.

Sarah Sails for St Petersburg

By this time there had been a drastic change in Sarah Kilham's life. For once we hear about this from Sarah herself, who surely underplays the drama of it. It was as early as 1819 that she learned about the opportunity in Russia, and Hannah encouraged her to grasp it:

> In 1819 it was my precious mother who first proposed my leaving England, and this she was led to do from an expression of countenance she observed in me, when a friend mentioned a person being wanted in Russia for girls' schools on the system of mutual instruction. She made every encouragement for this step with the utmost cheerfulness and alacrity, talked with interest of the new field of occupation, &c.[93]

Yet for some unknown reason it was apparently not until the summer of 1820 that William Allen put her name forward. On 16 August he recorded: 'Sarah Kilham is preparing to sail for Petersburg. I am busily employed in assisting her and in writing to some of my friends of that country'.[94] Next he wrote to V. M. Popov, head of the Department of Education under Golitsyn and chief escort on their visit:

> At that time we did not know of a suitable female to recommend who was acquainted with the new system, though I wrote to our committee in London to look out for such a person, well knowing that if they could find one in all respects adapted to your circumstances she would be invaluable to you. I think I may now say that such a one has providentially offered. Sarah Kilham, a young woman well known to the family of Daniel Wheeler, has thought it her religious duty to go to Petersburg and offer her services to conduct a model school for two or three hundred poor girls, provided that the Emperor would be pleased to sanction it. She goes out by the *Paris*, the vessel that carries this letter; she is highly respected at Sheffield...

Sarah tells a class at Leavy Greave School about her plans.

Then follows the remark previously quoted about Sarah's keeping a very successful school there. Allen goes on:

...but she thought it right to sacrifice everything to the present apprehension of duty; her mother, Hannah Kilham, is a highly useful and pious character. I am sure that if dear Grellet were present he would join me in earnestly requesting Prince Galitzin *(sic)* to mention the case to the Emperor; the motives of the young woman are, I believe, wholly disinterested, and I know that she is capable of being a blessing to your country. If the Emperor and the Empress mother were to encourage the measure, it would be easy to find ladies who would support such a school; this would be a central point, and mistresses might be trained here for all the Empire. I should have said that the young woman has, I believe, a pretty good knowledge of French.[95]

Thus William Allen keeps alive the notion of Sarah's starting a model school with a teacher training function. The afterthought about French was probably a deliberate point made in Sarah's favour, since French as the court language was the preferred medium of Alexander,[96] though he also had a good command of English.

Questions perhaps arise. Given that Alexander had already asked for a person to be supplied, and Sarah was shortly to be on her way, Allen's language seems strangely tentative; why? It may be because she did not exactly fit the bill, for Alexander had had a wider vision, wanting someone to organize or at least advise on setting up a Russian school society like the BFSS and interested in prison reform. But Allen's language is also explained if for 'tentative' we substitute 'deferential'. It also may appear odd, if Sarah heard the call in 1819, that Allen made no approach to the Russians until mid-August 1820. Again there may be the suitability factor, but another explanation could be that she did not inform him or confirm her offer until the future management of Leavy Greave School had been clarified. A third question, which undermines the premise of the first, is why a practical and to all appearances sensible 31-year-old teacher should leave for a distant unknown land with no more than a vague assurance of work. We shall return to that after taking a last look at the Sheffield situation.

By 1814 Sarah's stepmother Hannah was corresponding with William Allen, sharing as she did his social, educational and missionary interests, including the African Institution set up a few years earlier to 'promote the civilisation of Africa' and focussing on the liberated slaves of Sierra Leone. She was influenced by him. Allen and Grellet were unusual among the Quakers of their day in that they wanted to spread the Light abroad when the prevailing ethos was quietist, averse to seeking converts.[97] On 5 December she wrote in her diary:

> Are not Friends particularly called upon to act as school-missionaries, since they might do this in conformity with their best principles? And might they not in each place or station have meetings for religious worship?[98]

James Montgomery, no Quaker himself, put a sympathetic gloss on her views: rather than to evangelize by preaching, the goal would be to instruct through schools, thus enabling those taught to teach others in turn.[99] As the contemporary Quaker leadership saw it, however, ministry and mission expressed in educational projects did not sit easily together. Missionaries would normally require financial support. Ministers were, strictly, Friends who had been formally recognized as having a call to speak – Hannah would be so recognized by Balby Meeting in 1821 – but they were not paid.[100] Hannah's desire to reconcile two Quaker irreconcilables led at worst to a condemnatory view by the Society's leaders, though expressed in the mildest terms. In one of Greenwood's memorable judgments: 'Her ministry and doctrine, in their eyes, were tainted with the Methodism from which she came'.[101] What they had in mind not least was Methodism's evangelistic imperative.

The details of Hannah Kilham's increasing and life-changing commitment to West African education at home and in the field are available elsewhere.[102] This is what drew her to London for the winter of 1819-20. It proved to be a long winter, for apparently she did not return to Yorkshire until June 1820.[103] Sarah was on the verge of going to Russia. She and Hannah had been in touch over the preceding six months about current and future concerns, their own and their school's, but none of this correspondence appears to have survived. All we know is that Sarah made a will and in a separate document authorized Hannah to receive the interest on a sum of £500 belonging to her.[104]

HANNAH KILHAM

WITH respectful acknowledgment of the kindness of her Friends, informs them that the School at Leavy Greave will, after Midsummer, be conducted by ANN CORBETT and LUCY CROSS, for *Girls only*.

Leavy Greave, 5th Mo. 12th, 1821

Hannah continued the school for the 1820/21 session,[105] but then announced that she was transferring operations to her niece Ann – who had previously run it with Sarah – and Lucy Cross,[106] a young woman of eighteen from Ipswich who had attended Ackworth School from 1812 to

1816.[107] Perhaps this was intended as a temporary arrangement. At any rate, in July 1822, when Hannah's home base was at Tottenham, London, the school was in the hands of Quakers Mary and Rebecca Brady.[108] (A rare survival from the 1831 census reveals that Mary Brady remained in charge. It also indicates the size of the school family – 7 males and 21 females – though if the criterion 'resident population' was strictly observed this would exclude any day pupils.)[109] The Brady sisters were still running the school twenty years later.[110] Meanwhile Lucy Cross had worked as a governess, married Henry Waterfall of Leeds, been widowed with an infant son after eighteen months, set up her own successful school in Leeds and become a Quaker minister.[111]

Hannah usually exerted great self-control, so much that even Sarah, while not doubting her love, felt that their parting would not be painful for her. As the day came nearer, however, she gave vent to her emotions, but recovered her composure to see Sarah off at the quayside.[112] Sarah recorded nothing of her own feelings at this time. They were both strong, determined women. To some degree Hannah had moulded Sarah in her own image, and it was largely under the older woman's influence, one suspects, that the younger had been fired with missionary zeal. To see people go off into the unknown or barely known with little assurance of returning was not a rare experience; in 1817 Hannah's other niece Sarah Collier and her husband had sailed for Sierra Leone and both had died there.[113] The missionary impulse quenched doubts and assuaged fears, and this surely it was that enabled Sarah to sail for Russia with the object of running a school that so far existed only in the form of imagined pictures and spoken promises.

Notes and References

1 J.W. Graham, 'The Father of the Founder of the "Manchester Guardian"', *Journal of the Friends Historical Society*, 18 (1921), p 87, quoting John Taylor to Thomas Thompson of Dorset, Jun 1804. Taylor was the first master of Manchester Friends' School.

2 The historian of Quaker education curiously does not mention a Liverpool Friends' School at this date. The one for poor children in Duncan Street did not begin until 1816. Penketh, some fifteen miles away, intermittently had a private Quaker day school. Penketh School, a separate concern from this, operated from 1834 until 1934 (J.S. Hodgson, *A History of Penketh School, 1834-1907* (London, 1907), p 14; W.A.C. Stewart, *Quakers and Education* (London, 1953), pp 67, 69-70; M.M. Shearer, *Quakers in Liverpool* (Liverpool, 1982), p 18).

3 MCL: M85/5/15/1, entry for 8 Nov 1795.

4 MCL: M85/5/15/3.

5 The basis for this calculation and subsequent similar ones is the purchasing power of the pound, using the retail price index. Exact rates were obtained from www.measuringworth.com, accessed on various occasions in 2008, but instead of quoting them precisely for 2007, the latest year then available, it was decided to round them up for 2008. See Officer, L.H., in the List of Sources.
6 MCL: M85/5/15/3.
7 MCL: M85/5/15/1.
8 MCL: M85/5/15/3.
9 Biller, ed., p 90; Ward, p 196; Dickson, p 75.
10 M. Walton, *Sheffield: Its Story and its Achievements* (Sheffield, 1948), p 103.
11 *The Iris*, 30 Dec 1806 (cp. 10 and 17 July).
12 M. Howitt, *An Autobiography*, 1 (London, 1889), p 85; J.O. Greenwood, *Quaker Encounters, 2: Vines on the Mountains* (York, 1977), p 100.
13 MCL: M85/2/7/1, f 47; M85/2/7/2, f 23; MFPR 938.
14 *List of the Boys and Girls admitted into Ackworth School 1779 to 1879* (Ackworth and London, 1879), p 55.
15 *Sheffield Society for Bettering the Condition and Increasing the Comfort of the Poor: 6th Report* (1809), p 2 (hereafter *Sheffield Bettering Society*); from: www.institutions.org.uk/poor_law_unions/sheffield_society.htm
16 Friends House Library (FHL): 033.9664, Kilham Box; *Sheffield Mercury* (henceforth *SM*), 27 June and 4 July 1812.
17 Howitt, p 87.
18 Ibid.
19 Hoare, pp 77, 110; D.M. Butler, *The Quaker Meeting Houses of Britain*, 2 (London, 1999), pp 833-4; H.E. Roberts, *Researching Yorkshire Quaker History* (Hull, 2003), p 64.
20 Stone, p 232.
21 FHL: Ms 156/123 (Spriggs I), HK to Frances Thompson, 5 Aug 1819.
22 *SM*, 18 Jan 1812. On 27 June his advertisement follows hers.
23 Dickson, p 75.
24 Derived from rates for 2007 at www.measuringworth.com, accessed in 2008.
25 J. Dunstan, *Dore Old School in Records and Recollections* (Sheffield, 2006), p 9 (derived).
26 Howitt, p 85.
27 FHL: 'Dictionary of Quaker Biography' (typescript files).
28 Birmingham Central Library: Cadbury Collection, Ms 466/94, Candia Barrow to George and Elizabeth Barrow, 6 Aug 1819. She gives an account of her coach journey back to school.
29 I.A. Williams, *The Firm of Cadbury 1831-1931* (London, 1931), pp 5-6, 12.
30 Howitt, p 85.
31 Ibid., pp 85-6.
32 Dickson, p 75.
33 FHL: Ms 156/123 (Spriggs I), HK to Frances Thompson, 5 Aug 1819. Listing shoes (for indoor wear?) were made of selvedge (cloth edging).
34 *SM*, 27 Feb 1819. This makes it clear that the address is new.
35 Dickson, p 111.

36 *Life of William Allen with Selections from his Correspondence*, 3 vols (London, 1846-7), 2, p 182 (henceforth *Allen*).

37 SA: QR 8, Balby Monthly Meeting, Minutes, 1806-1814, p 58.

38 Ibid., p 68.

39 Ibid., p 139.

40 SA: QR 105, Minutes of the Sub-Committee on the Poor's Account, *passim*.

41 Dickson, pp 65-70 (for a full account); Biller, ed., p 102.

42 Holland and Everett, 3, pp 246-7.

43 *Sheffield Bettering Society*, p 2.

44 Derived from rates for 2007 at www.measuringworth.com, accessed in 2008.

45 *SM*, 14 Aug 1819 and 10 Mar 1821.

46 Dickson, pp 71-3.

47 Ibid., p 105; Twells, '"Let us begin well"', p 33.

48 Ward, p 196.

49 *SM*, 7 and 14 Jan 1815, 17 Feb 1816, 15 Feb 1817, 4 Mar 1820, 24 Feb 1821, 2 Mar 1822.

50 Dickson, p 96 ff; Twells, '"Let us begin well"', p 25.

51 Biller, ed., pp 142-68; Dickson, pp 130, 132-8; Twells, '"Let us begin well"', pp 36-40.

52 *Report of the British and Foreign School Society (BFSS)*, 17 (1822), p 163, and successive years to 22 (1827), p 158.

53 Ward, p 281.

54 *SM*, 18 Jan 1817, 14 Aug 1819.

55 *SM*, 14 Jan 1815, 17 Feb 1816.

56 J. Taylor, *Joseph Lancaster: The Poor Child's Friend* (West Wickham, 1996), provides more information than the standard histories of English education.

57 Ibid., p 40.

58 Dickson, p 80; Taylor, pp 79-80.

59 Ibid., pp 91, 93-6, 98.

60 *Allen*, 1, pp 94-170 *passim*; here p 191.

61 *SM*, 7 and 14 Jan and 4 Nov 1815.

62 *SM*, 17 Feb 1816.

63 *SM*, 15 Feb and 23 Aug 1817, 28 Feb 1818.

64 Biller, ed., p 121.

65 *SM*, 4 Mar 1820, 24 Feb 1821, 2 Mar 1822.

66 FHL: Ms 156/123 (Spriggs I), HK to Frances Thompson, 5 Aug 1819; her emphasis.

67 *SM*, 19 June 1819.

68 B. Hollingsworth, 'Lancasterian Schools in Russia', *Durham Research Review*, 5, no 17 (1966), pp 59-60; J.C. Zacek, 'The Lancastrian School Movement in Russia', *Slavonic and East European Review*, 45 (1967), pp 345-6.

69 *Allen*, 1, pp 193-201; Scott, pp 52-5.

70 Taylor, p 21.

71 *Allen*, 1, pp 206-8, 253-4.

72 Ibid., pp 290, 306; Hollingsworth, pp 61-2; Zacek, p 347.

73 Hollingsworth, pp 62-3, 65-6; Zacek, pp 346, 348.

74 *Report of the BFSS*, 18 (1823), p 98.

75 *Allen*, 1, pp 359, 420-48 (to end of 1818); Hollingsworth, p 65; Zacek, pp 349, 351; Scott, pp 84-6; and on Paterson: H. Pitcher, *Muir & Mirrielees* (Cromer, 1994), pp 7-8.

76 R.E. Leader, ed., *Reminiscences of Old Sheffield* (Sheffield, 1876), pp 53, 317-18.

77 SA: QR 34, Register of Births, Sheffield, 1795-1822.

78 Cited in W.J. Townsend, H.B. Workman and G. Eayrs, ed., *A New History of Methodism*, 1 (London, 1909), p 529.

79 SA: QR 34, Register of Births, Sheffield, 1795-1822.

80 On The Hill in Quaker history see Hoare, pp 71-2.

81 Scott, pp 57-67; Greenwood, 2, pp 117, 123-30.

82 Not Volkov (ibid., p 128), which is a town 100 miles to the east.

83 J.B. [Benson], *From the Lune to the Neva Sixty Years Ago* (London, 1879), pp 52-3, 62, 68-72, 87 (names are thinly disguised: 'William Doubleday' is William Singleton, 'John Skelton' is George Edmondson, 'Hallam' is Sheffield, 'Heatherly Hall' is Broomhall); Greenwood, 2, p 126; Scott, p 63. George was on the Ackworth roll from 1810 to 1811 (*List of the Boys and Girls*, p 71).

84 Sheffield City Libraries, *A Guide to the Fairbank Collection* (Sheffield, 1936), pp 5-6. Greenwood, 2, pp 126-7, describes him as George's fellow-lodger at the school, but being about six years younger he may have been a pupil. He had been at Ackworth from 1815 to 1816 (*List of the Boys and Girls*, p 82).

85 [Benson], pp 88-114; Greenwood, 2, pp 126-34; Scott, pp 62-73.

86 Hollingsworth, pp 63-4.

87 S.B. Paina, 'Peterburgskaya shkola Vol'nogo obshchestva uchrezhdeniya uchilishch vzaimnogo obucheniya (1819-1825)', *Novye issledovaniya v pedagogicheskikh naukakh* (hereafter *NIPN*), 7 (20) (1973), pp 11-12.

88 *Allen*, 2, p 3; Hollingworth, pp 68-9; Scott, p 92.

89 *Allen*, 1, p 467, and 2, p 6.

90 Ibid., 2, p 14.

91 Ibid., 2, p 66; Zacek, pp 350, 352-3; Scott, pp 89, 90-2. The inaugural date of the Committee is given by Hollingsworth as 1820.

92 Calculated from table and other data in Hollingsworth, p 64, citing a report of 1823 in V. Bazanov, *Uchenaya respublika* (Moscow and Leningrad, 1964), p 18.

93 Biller, ed., p 128.

94 *Allen*, 2, p 180.

95 Ibid., 2, p 182.

96 R. Hingley, *The Tsars* (London, 1968, 1973), p 185.

97 Dickson, pp 95-7. Especially Grellet: see Sykes, pp 189-99.

98 Biller, ed., p 148.

99 Holland and Everett, 3, p 246.

100 Dickson, pp 96, 122.

101 Greenwood, 2, p 114.

102 Dickson's biography is supplemented on this topic by a study by A. Twells, '"So Distant and Wild a Scene": Language, Domesticity and Difference in Hannah Kilham's Writing from West Africa, 1822-1832', *Women's History Review*, 4 (1995), pp 301-18.

103 Dickson, pp 111, 116.
104 The National Archives (TNA): Prob 11/1810 f 262 (will of Hannah Kilham, citing Sarah's).
105 *SM*, 17 June 1820.
106 *SM*, 26 May 1821.
107 *List of the Boys and Girls*, p 76.
108 *SM*, 13 July 1822. It was still in the extended Quaker family: Daniel Wheeler's wife Jane was a Brady of Thorne, and a Rebecca Brady (the same?) had been among his party to Russia in 1818 (Greenwood, 2, pp 118, 126).
109 SA: CA 21 (25), Nether Hallam, Sheffield, Census, 'Formula for Taking and Preparing the Account…', 30 May [-4 June] 1831 (with thanks to Martin Olive).
110 Census returns, 1851, from: www.ancestrylibrary.com
111 FHL: 'Dictionary of Quaker Biography'. She gave up the school about 1863 and died in 1885.
112 Biller, ed., pp 128-9.
113 Dickson, p 98.

3. FOUNDING A SCHOOL

SARAH'S FIRST RUSSIAN DECADE

Arrival at Okhta

CERTAINLY THE cautious, sober Daniel Wheeler had no sympathy for what he regarded as impulsive behaviour based on ignorance. He seems to have been taken aback when Sarah appeared on his doorstep at Okhta. Had it all been arranged in such a rush that William Allen had had no opportunity to warn him? Moreover, it was irritating that due Quaker process had not yet been observed. She was already there by 7 September 1820, when George Edmondson wrote to his father, 'Not many days ago a female friend of ours arrived from Sheffield, her object is to establish a Lancastrian school for girls, under government'.[1] About the same time Balby Monthly Meeting issued a certificate of her removal to St Petersburg and to their outpost ('Allowed Meeting') at Okhta,[2] but receipt of the document in Russia was not minuted and acknowledged until January 1821:

> Our friend Sarah Kilham having removed from Sheffield to Petersburgh, we hereby inform you on her behalf, that upon inquiry it appears she has left us free from debt or any engagement relating to marriage, and was of orderly conduct. – In removing thus far from her Native Land, under the prospect of an arduous engagement, we feel a tender solicitude that her movements may be under the direction of best Wisdom, and that she may be favoured to experience preservation and a growth in the Truth; we therefore affectionately recommend her to your tender notice and regard, and are with the salutation of love your friends.[3]

Meanwhile Daniel Wheeler had written impatiently:

> Why did she come out? We knew nothing of her coming here, no prospects for her employment, though she is very agreeable to the young folks and useful to their learning... If she had written [to me] she would not have left home without certain information that neither dear William nor her *(sic)* were in possession of.[4]

Wheeler had now been living in Russia for over two years, quite long enough to become aware – despite his favoured treatment – of the delays and prevarications of the Russian bureaucracy, and possibly of incipient opposition to Lancasterian schools in some official quarters. Ironically, this had been sparked off by Allen's and Grellet's intervention over the irreligious – and thus perceived as subversive – curriculum content of the military ones. (In October a mutiny would lead to an investigation, the sacking of the director of regimental schools and some closures.)[5] Moreover, according to Greenwood, matters were not helped by William Allen's 'tactless instructions' that Sarah should go to the Venning brothers when she needed money'.[6] The instructions were sensible given that Allen had a good understanding with the Vennings and they could well afford it, but Wheeler disliked them. They were not Quakers. For all their generous philanthropy he found them too worldly, and it may well have rankled that Allen and Grellet had preferred their company to his, though he had missed them after they left. John Venning had recently become more seriously religious but the damage had been done.[7]

Sarah arrives at Kronstadt, then the port of St Petersburg.

Sarah Kilham was popular with the four young Wheelers, Sarah (13), Charles (nearly 11), Daniel junior (soon 8) and Jane or Jenny (4). George Edmondson gives news of her progress up to 5 December:

> The young woman I mentioned who is come with the intention of establishing a school for girls on the Lancastrian plan is at present lodging with us; whilst work was open she took charge of the children which was a great relief to me *[because he could turn his full attention to land reclamation before winter set in]*. The Emperor is at

present from home but he has been informed of her arrival, & wishes her to attend to the acquisition of the language. The establishment of such a school as the one proposed has long been an object he has wished to accomplish and [he] expresses himself much pleased with the present opportunity. We have been expecting his return some time.[8]

Daniel Wheeler's less sanguine expectations were justified: Sarah had to wait and wait. William Allen asked him to convey to her his sympathy, his hope that she would not be discouraged, and his conviction of great and good consequences once the Emperor had returned. Meanwhile Sarah was putting her enforced leisure to good use, firstly to learn Russian,[9] as Alexander had commanded, and secondly to acclimatize herself to the Russian winter. The extreme cold brought wolves closer than usual to places where people lived, making it dangerous for the Wheelers to go out at night, so they stayed indoors.[10] As for the weather itself, here is a rare domestic cameo sent by George to his sister the following March:

> SK went out one morning just to breathe the fresh air, at the time there were 24 deg. of frost & a high wind, the cold was terrible. She had not gone a hundred yards before her nose was frozen, from this you may have some idea, though a very imperfect one, of the degree of cold here.[11]

I have myself experienced exactly these conditions in St Petersburg, also in March. My nose survived intact, but I found the combination of cold and wind literally breathtaking and had to retreat indoors to get my breath back.

It would be interesting to know how Sarah went about learning the language. She was just too early for the two Russian grammars for English speakers that appeared in the 1820s, the later and superior one by James Heard.[12] Perhaps, however, he had briefed William Allen on what was available. There were only two works. One was the London publication *A Commercial Dictionary of the English and Russian Languages* (1800?), by Adam Kroll, which James Muckle demonstrates to be 'grotesque'. If Sarah had seen it in time, though, it would at least have alerted her to the possibility of her luggage being temporarily impounded! The other was Nikolai Grammatin's huge *New Dictionary English and Russian*, published in Moscow in 1808.[13] It is highly likely that Daniel Wheeler and his household possessed this, and given his key work for government since 1818 he was surely in a position to secure efficient tutoring.

Sarah's New School and Richard Knill's

Late in the summer, after nearly a year's wait, Sarah's dream began to be realized. On 8 September William Allen made this entry in his diary:

I received a very important letter this morning from John Venning, of Petersburg, stating that the Emperor had granted an audience to Sarah Kilham, and had decided to establish a girls' school, upon the British system, and that S.K. had also been introduced to the Empress Elizabeth, who had agreed to become the patroness. Thus this great object seems in a fair way to be accomplished.[14]

'British', from the British and Foreign School Society, means Lancasterian. The BFSS referred to Sarah, though not by name, in its next report: its Committee had had 'the satisfaction of providing and sending out a Mistress for a School for Girls, to be formed in St Petersburg'.[15]

The school was opened later in 1821. This date is from Sarah's own pen, as is our earliest detail of the school's history: 'Initially ten poor girls were selected by the Imperial Philanthropic Society and are fully maintained [by them]'.[16] Allen had wanted the Imperial Philanthropic Society, with Golitsyn as its President, to be the agency for setting up Lancasterian schools.[17] This did not happen, but their sponsorship of the first ten pupils was a significant start. According to an almost contemporary Russian report, the school opened in October 1821 with 50 girls aged 8-12.[18] This probably means enrolment rather than attendance. It presents no contradiction if day-pupils and further boarders accounted for the difference, as they certainly did four years later. Annual fees, said to be low, are quoted for both: 12 roubles for day-pupils, 225 for boarders.[19] The mere fact of quoting fees at all hints that there was no wish to present the school exclusively as an institution for poor people.

Another point seems to have been of greater concern to Allen and was probably made by him in letters of 19 and 24 October 1821 which Sarah either never received or chose to ignore: 'I long to hear that her school has become a training establishment for mistresses – the plan of a boarding school I never liked – but the [Lancasterian] system has enemies'.[20] The enemies evidently included two members – D.P. Runich and M.L. Magnitsky – of the small Special Committee for the Establishment of Schools of Mutual Instruction mentioned earlier![21] As an intelligent man Allen could scarcely believe that the course of Russia's educational development depended solely on his close personal friendship with some of its prime movers, but sometimes his writing sounds as if he did believe it. Here he shows a more realistic attitude.

Nevertheless Allen received more satisfying news in 1822. In January John Venning came to London with a favourable report on Sarah, who in addition to her more direct responsibilities had helped him to set up a school 'for the poor little foreign boys who used to be begging about the streets; they now amount to about seventy'.[22] This school had been opened on 17/29 October 1821 by the Rev Richard Knill (1787-1857). He was a young Congregational minister appointed to St Petersburg by the London Missionary Society (LMS) at the request of John Paterson of the BFBS to serve the English-speaking Protestant nonconformist community. They met in the chapel of the German-speaking United Brethren, or Moravians, a church which broke with Rome in 1467. Knill tells us that the original idea came from a Mr Gray, one of his congregation, which also included the Venning brothers. Walter had asked Gray to visit a prison and read – and presumably explain – the Scriptures to an inmate. This activity appealed to Gray and led him to suggest to John Venning the notion of a school for poor foreigners. Venning mentioned this to Knill,[23] who drew up a document explaining the plan for the school and soliciting public aid. Venning took it to the evangelical Princess Meshcherskaya (whom we shall meet again shortly) to be translated, and she interceded with the Emperor, who happened to call. She told him that she had often heard Knill preach.

Subsequently Prince Golitsyn informed Venning that the Emperor had not only approved the project but allocated a start-up grant of 5000 roubles. He had appointed Knill superintendent with a salary of 2000 roubles a year. The master, none other than Mr Gray, was to receive 1000 roubles a year.[24] On the face of it, these sums appear quite generous, assuming that the exchange rate of 1821 was reasonably close to that of 1816 (4s 6d to the rouble)[25] and that it was a fair rate in terms of purchasing power. By this token 1000 roubles would have amounted to £225 in 1821, equivalent to over £16,000 in 2008.[26] James Heard, back in St Petersburg, evidently gave Gray practical advice on the Lancasterian system, which he gladly adopted. Heard called it 'a German school with about 130 boys'.[27] Soon girls were admitted and a mistress was also employed.[28]

Extolling the system, the first report of the school stated:

> Here we see two hundred children of both sexes instructed with astonishing rapidity, under the direction of two persons, on the most moderate terms. And a much greater number might be taught at the same expense.[29]

There were 170 boys and 70 girls on the roll in August 1823.[30] By November 1826 pupils numbered 233 boys and 178 girls, two-thirds of them Germans. The list of 58 subscriptions included 25 roubles per year from Sarah Kilham,[31] who was also appointed to its committee of management.[32] This school is quite well documented, but Sarah seems to have been involved only on its periphery and we shall not go further into its story for fear of confusion with that of her own school and another for boys about to be mentioned. The point to stress is that the school superintended by Richard Knill was for poor *foreign* children, whereas Sarah's and a parallel boys' school were for young *Russians*.

James Heard's Model School

Yet more good news now reached William Allen. On 26 May 1822 he recorded in his diary: 'A nephew of H. Kilham's arrived from Petersburg, and brought me a letter from Sarah Kilham, with a good account of her school'.[33] This was either William or Henry Spurr, sons of Hannah's brother Peter; it was probably the former, who had a business in St Petersburg and was then aged about 24, whereas Henry was a 14-year-old schoolboy there.[34] Next came a letter from John Venning, containing what appears to be our earliest notice of a scheme which would have turned the Kilham project into part of what the BFSS devoutly wished:

> For your information, and that of your committee, I have the pleasure to send you herewith an extract of a letter received yesterday from His Excellency Mr Papof *[Golitsyn's secretary and Director of Public Education V.M. Popov]* relative to the school for poor Russian boys. I have given in the outline of a plan for the establishment of a model school for two hundred boys and two hundred girls; the boys to be under the superintendence of Mr Heard, the girls under Miss Kilham. It will be laid before His Majesty in a few days...[35]

Venning did not find it advisable to mention something of which Allen was possibly aware: the opposition, presumably on religious grounds, of a pamphleteering French priest, whose efforts he himself strove to counteract.[36]

So James Heard, who had returned to England to see his mother and had most likely been working temporarily as a Lancasterian school inspector under William Allen's direction, was about to embark on his second Russian venture. In March 1822 Allen, in a letter to Wheeler, had referred to this without needing to specify what was already at the planning stage: '...there is some probability that James Heard, a nice young man who understands our System of Education and speaks Russ, will go to Petersburg by the first ship... I propose to write to James shortly'.[37] Soon the BFSS was able to inform its members: 'Mr Heard, who acquitted himself so much to the satisfaction of Count Romanzoff on his mission to the extensive estates of His Excellency at Homel, is now on his way to the capital of Russia'.[38]

The Emperor Alexander decided in July 1822 to establish the school.[39] Readers of the BFSS Report for 1823 were able to chart the course of developments from James Heard's own news bulletins. On 22 October he wrote: 'His Imperial Majesty has confirmed the estimate of expenses, and granted 7000 roubles per annum for the support of a Model School in

Petersburg; as soon as a convenient place can be found and fitted up, it will be opened'.[40] From other sources we learn that this followed a start-up grant of 10,000 roubles and was accompanied by an annual allocation of 3000 roubles for James's salary as school principal.[41] Three months later James wrote again: 'I am now fitting up the school in grand style, in hopes that it may become a Model School, and that the government will adopt the system in all the common schools in the empire; which is by no means improbable'. And finally on 10 May 1823, after what must have been a fiercely busy six weeks, he put pen to paper once more: 'I now have the pleasure of informing you that I have opened a large school for 200 boys... Twenty-five scholars were admitted on the 1st of April; and the number has been gradually increasing till now, though we have but 75'.[42] The age-range was from 7 to 12.[43] By September, with 107 boys, the school was half full.[44]

The BFSS spelled out for its supporters what James Heard had meant by a model school: 'An opportunity will thus be afforded for the training of masters, by whose means the system of mutual instruction will gradually convey the blessings of knowledge to every district of that extensive empire'.[45] Although this would be realized to a modest extent, it betokened pious hope rather than Russian reality. The naturally optimistic William Allen had been told the whole truth in April 1823 when visited by the Bible Society's agent Robert Pinkerton: during the Emperor's five months' absence abroad in 1822-23 'there had been opposition at all points to the Bible Society, schools, &c.; and poor Heard's patience had been tried to the utmost'. Only the Emperor's intervention from Verona had cleared the way.[46] This opposition was political and religious, with a government and a church *a priori* suspicious of subversive ideas, un-Orthodox views and foreigners. Perhaps this was what drove John Venning to look (in vain) for a suitable young man to replace James Heard. Reports to the BFSS had to be upbeat, but he privately felt that the school's progress was slow.[47] Although the Bible Society and the Lancasterian movement both claimed to be non-sectarian, they were widely perceived as foreign and Protestant.

It is interesting to note the membership of the management committee of James's school: Venning, his German-born wife Julia, S.S. Dzhunkovsky, who, as we shall see, was to play a still more important role in Sarah's school, Sarah herself, Princess Meshcherskaya – and a certain Runich whom we have met before.[48] In this context the last three names, taken in reverse order, prompt reflection. Recording John Venning's 'persevering zeal' in thwarting hostility to the school project, Thulia Henderson proceeds to note, without obvious irony, that 'formal sanction to the entire plan was given through His Excellency M. Runitsch [Runich], the curator of all seminaries for public instruction'.[49] Whether such a deadpan statement conveys ignorance or conceals amusement is impossible to say. These events had taken place forty years earlier, but Venning had died only four years before publication of the *Memorials* in 1862.

As members of the government Committee for the Establishment of Schools of Mutual Instruction, Runich and his colleague M.L. Magnitsky had opposed the Free Society set up for that purpose, investigated its schools and attempted to close it down. They had also attacked the Central Pedagogical Institute, responsible for training Lancasterian teachers, on the charge of spreading the ideas of J.H. Pestalozzi and misapplying the Lancasterian method.[50] Certainly the agents of the autocratic state had problems with the Swiss reformer who held that teachers should help children to develop individually through enjoyable activity and encourage them to think for themselves in a setting of gently controlled freedom. At some point the Committee was renamed 'Committee for the Supervision of Lancasterian Schools of Mutual Instruction', and this was realistic, for it established none of its own accord.[51]

Having worn down the Free Society's St Petersburg school by interfering in the teaching process – from 1824 all schools of mutual instruction had to follow the parish school syllabuses in the three Rs and RI – the members of the Supervisory Committee would not even take over its funding (and thereby increase their control) when asked to do so by a dispirited Free Society Committee chairman in 1825.[52] They preferred to watch it die. Defeated by government hostility and financial stringency, the Free Society Committee wound up both the Society and its school, on a temporary basis which became permanent.[53] Runich, then, was the potentially vicious watchdog on James Heard's management committee. But it is only fair to add that a scholar who has looked at him more closely declines to tar him with exactly the same brush as Magnitsky. He follows the general line on Magnitsky's shameless careerism but sees Runich primarily as a dour reactionary.[54]

D.P. Runich, critic of Lancasterian schools.

Princess Sof'ya Sergeevna Meshcherskaya (1775-1848) is characterized in the main title of a study by Wendy Rosslyn, 'Benevolent Ladies and their Exertions for the Good of Humankind',[55] and she figures prominently in it. We also meet her repeatedly in William Allen's record of his Russian visit. She had a favoured background: her father was very wealthy and her mother a lady-in-waiting at court. Having had an Orthodox upbringing, in 1811 she was converted to evangelical Christianity under the spiritual direction of the former missionary Robert Pinkerton, appointed tutor to her children.[56] She became a close friend of Alexander I and, in Stephen Grellet's Quakerly terms, 'She was God's instrument in supporting a religious disposition in the soul of the Emperor, when he first experienced the powerful influence of the spirit of truth'.[57] Her Christian faith led her to devote the rest of her life to good causes. Fluent in English, she spent much time and money on the translation and distribution of religious tracts (on which more later). She was a hands-on member of the Ladies' Committee of the Society for the Care of Prisons (1818), serving as President from 1823 to 1826. In 1818 she had assisted Walter Venning in his initial prison-visiting and in translating his report to the Emperor with its reform proposals.[58]

This is an illustration of Meshcherskaya's role of intermediary; in Rosslyn's words, a call on her 'became a standard part of the initiation' of English-speakers into Russian philanthropic circles.[59] Another case in point was that of Grellet and Allen, who went to see her in their first week in Russia. 'I spoke to her on the subject of the education of the poor', wrote Allen, 'and she is willing to take the lead in the female department'.[60] At nearly all their subsequent meetings they discussed schools, and on New Year's Eve 1818 she expressed her strongest commitment yet: '...we had much conversation about a girls' school here, upon our plan; she is earnestly bent upon having one, and has no doubt of procuring the Emperor's sanction'.[61] She later obtained the consent of A.P. Kozodavleva, the Minister of the Interior's widow, to become president of the school committee. On 23 March she asked Allen 'to write immediately for a school-mistress', whom she would take into her own family. Three weeks later he wrote to her from Moscow enclosing what sounds like a final draft of 'the plan for the girls' school'.[62]

Given all these undertakings, it is strange that Meshcherskaya's name then vanished from Allen's record of his negotiations about schools, though they remained friends and occasionally corresponded.[63] She was never mentioned by Sarah in relation to her own school either. Not knowing what went on behind the scenes, we cannot even be sure that Meshcherskaya's request of 23 March 1819 was a crucial factor in Sarah's appointment, though in view of her closeness to Alexander it is certainly a possibility. Despite her promise, Sarah was not taken into her family and it seems that no committee under Kozodavleva emerged. What is a matter of fact is that they had opportunities to meet through service on the committees of the other two schools, and they evidently became friends.[64]

Sarah is silent on her role on James Heard's committee and also on Richard Knill's school management body. (Thulia Henderson describes the women members – they were the same on both committees – in Lancasterian terms as lady-visitors.[65]) In fact the silence goes much further. The last time James Heard speaks of collaboration with Sarah or of provision for girls is in 1822, probably in July, just after receiving the Emperor's go-ahead: 'Miss Kilham's school is to be connected with that for boys, and the whole is to be called the central or model school'.[66] Otherwise his reports on his school to the BFSS are expressed in terms of his sole responsibility for his own creation.

Allen followed up Venning's letter about the proposed model school when he met the Emperor in Vienna on 1 October 1822: 'we spoke of Sarah Kilham, with whose exertions he expressed himself perfectly satisfied. I recommended her school to be made a place for training pious young women as school-mistresses'.[67] Yet Sarah nowhere describes her school as, or as part of, a model school. Indeed, after the anonymous reference to 'a Mistress for a School for Girls', which we take to mean Sarah, in their 1821 *Report* noted earlier, the BFSS Committee never mention her directly or indirectly, whereas 'the Model School at St Petersburgh… superintended by Mr Heard' is recorded several times.[68] We have discovered no management committee for Sarah's school, with or without BFSS stalwarts, and we suspect that it was too much under the direct patronage of the Imperial Family for the BFSS to regard it as one of theirs. George Edmondson described it bluntly as 'a boarding & day school on the Lancasterian plan *belonging to the Emperor*'.[69] Presumably such considerations were behind Hollingsworth's comment that 'Venning's second venture *[the model school]*… was largely taken over by Heard'.[70]

Some of Sarah's Pupils

There is no evidence that Sarah herself was interested in running a model school with its important function of identifying and training future teachers through the monitorial system. As we shall see, some of her charges did become teachers, but that was by the by. She was more intent on teaching them, as she put it, 'all sorts of domestic business'[71] – the school was run on mutual-help principles, without indoor servants and with just two men as porters and gardeners – and that was in turn to keep them off the streets from which many had been taken. In her own words again: 'I wish for them to learn to act rightly from principle and love, not from a fear of punishment'.[72] In 1831 she would add an 'infant school' operating seven or eight hours a day, and later wrote, 'it is a great pleasure to me to be made the instrument of keeping these lambs from the streets and evil words, for the greater part of their [mothers'] working hours'.[73] Sarah's chief concern, then, was to bring up her children – several of them formerly destitute or deprived – in a safe and loving Christian environment, and it was the welfare function of her school that was paramount. Consequently its residential aspect stood out: earlier, in 1825, she was providing round-the-clock care for 27 of her pupils.[74]

What can be said about these girls, their backgrounds and their careers? Thanks to John Venning we know a little about six of them. Another form of philanthropic activity by British expatriates was prison-visiting. Walter Venning, back in England from 1807 to 1817, had become a Christian in 1810 and been won to the cause of prison reform. He had joined the new Society for the Improvement of Prison Discipline, founded in 1815 by famous names in his banking profession, Fry, Gurney and Hoare. On returning to the Russian capital, through John Paterson he met Prince Golitsyn and was commissioned to visit prisons and, as previously mentioned, report on the hellish conditions there to Alexander I. Next he inspired his brother to follow him, first into the prisons and then into the Church. In 1818 it was they who with the Emperor's blessing together formed the Society for the Care of Prisons. Early in 1821 after Walter's death from typhoid, most likely caught whilst visiting prisoners, John took over the baton. He engaged the interest and support of influential Russians and even the patronage of Nicholas I, until he and Julia moved back to England in 1830.[75]

The first pair of sisters, not named, were 8 and 13 years old, brought with their mother, the widow of an army captain, to the city prison when she was gaoled for debt. It must have been an unusually sad case, for the other women prisoners clubbed together to pay off the debt from their earnings. John Venning arranged for Sarah to take the children in: 'I sent the two little girls to Miss Kilham, who, with her usual readiness to assist the afflicted, received them both into her school'.[76]

One day in 1825 Venning and his friend Archibald Mirrielees went to visit a women's prison and saw a new inmate arriving with two children aged about 12 and 14. Questioning her, he found that she had been gaoled for robbery. Her husband had been exiled to Siberia and the girls had nobody else to look after them. She begged the two visitors to arrange for them to be cared for. So Mirrielees took them on a drozhki – droshkies, as the British called them, were low one-horse, two-passenger, four-wheeled open carriages, their wheels notoriously liable to fall off,[77] as numerous on the streets of St Petersburg then as taxis in London or cabs in New York now – 'to that kind-hearted Christian, Miss Kilham, who received them into her school, and brought them up in the nurture and admonition of the Lord'.[78]

In the aftermath of the Great Flood of 1824 Venning had been instrumental in opening two 'refuges' for poor people, one just for four months not far from Sarah's school and the other in the 4th Line on Vasil'evsky Island across the Neva. The latter was continued from public subscription. By 1826 it had over 80 residents and was moved to the 13th Line for a more airy situation. A small school was attached to it, providing religious instruction and later reading, writing and sewing.[79] In 1828 Venning needed a teacher and consulted Sarah. She replied that one of her best girls was the elder of the two they had sent from the prison three years earlier. They took her on, found her completely satisfactory – indeed she became 'quite a treasure' – and her sister followed her with similar good results.[80]

A third pair of sisters, Feodosia, 9 and Maria, 5, came upon the scene early in 1829. They were two of seven spied begging on the ice of the Neva by the Emperor, now Nicholas I, out for his drive before dinner. He gave orders that their cases be examined and asked Venning to do it. Venning established that five of them were peasant children and thus the responsibility of their owners. (Except in the Baltic, serfs were not freed

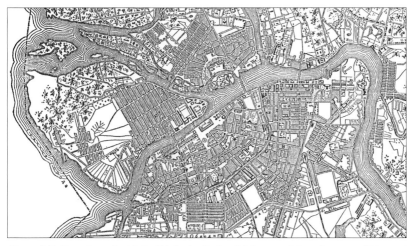

Map of St Petersburg in 1849 (Tsylov). Scale: 0.83 cm to 1 km (just over ½ in to 1 mile). The Neva flows NE to N, then bends SW, forking into the Bol'shaya Neva and the Malaya to the WNW. At the fork is the E tip of Vasil'evsky Island. To its NE, on a much smaller island, is the Peter & Paul Fortress (founded 1703), with Petrograd Side to the N. S of this, across the Neva, is the Hermitage complex, with the Winter Palace (1754-62) to the SW. Next, surrounded by the river and wide squares, is the Admiralty (1806-23). Sarah's area was further SW (see enlarged map). Okhta, where the Wheelers lived, is on the opposite side of the city, E of the Neva.

until 1861.) As for Feodosia and Maria, their father, a junior naval officer, was dead, their mother was too poor to maintain them, and so they had become beggars. Venning recommended that they be placed in Sarah's school. He knew that she had the capacity to admit them, attributing it to her skill in administering the annual government grant. This was agreed, and he himself took the little girls there.[81]

In October 1841 Sarah sent John Venning an update on Feodosia and Maria. Towards the end of the older girl's school career, Sarah suggested she stayed on as a teacher, but this did not appeal to her. So Feodosia went into service in the family of a Mr Nottbeck, a prosperous German merchant whose name crops up from time to time among foreign philanthropists. After some years she went to another family as a nanny, until marriage beckoned. Because of the mother's poverty, Sarah offered to host the reception at the school, provided that it was on a temperance basis; and so it was. Sarah was optimistic about the pair:

> The bride and bridegroom began their housekeeping altogether within their income; and he being sober, and with a good salary, and she neither dressy nor fond of visiting, they have every prospect of comfort, especially as both desire to live in the fear of the Lord.

This says as much about Sarah's principles and priorities as it does the young couple's: good with money, abstemious and God-fearing. Maria, meanwhile, had taken over the post of nanny from her sister.[82]

Coping with Crises

What do we know about the daily life of Sarah's school and of her own role as its head? The sparse records of the first few years of the school's activities mainly comprise brief and uninformative mentions of good progress. Then, however, something happened: a crisis which almost threatened the school's existence, a crisis to which Sarah's response portrays her in a heroic light and has already ensured her a niche in the annals of British people in Imperial Russia. As the location of the school played a defining part in this event, it would be good to begin with that, but we have a problem. The earliest specific address discovered for Sarah's school is much later (1849) though she refers to the same local area in a letter of 1841.[83] A very early source (1823) places her school in the Narva District,[84] which lay immediately south of the Admiralty District, 4th Section, where we know it was situated afterwards. In a letter of 1827 she refers to a large house outside the city with a fine fruit garden and another for vegetables.[85] Sarah nowhere mentions a removal, therefore we cannot date it. So as we go on to reconstruct the location of her school, we have to make a choice; and we prefer to depict the later area, emphasizing nevertheless the closeness of the earlier site and its exposure to exactly the same weather conditions on the edge of the Gulf of Finland. That St Petersburg has grown enormously since Sarah's time is no surprise. In her day the built-up area was confined to part of the two principal islands of the Neva delta – Petrograd Side (Petrogradskaya storona) to the north, the site of Peter the Great's first settlement, and Vasil'evsky Island (ostrov) to the west – and the mainland to the south as far as the Obvodny Canal.[86] After the Neva divides in its journey westwards and seawards to form the misshapen prongs of a fork, each with its own name, it is the southernmost prong which possesses most importance and thus the title Bol'shaya Neva, the Great Neva. Just before this river reaches the Gulf of Finland, with the southern tip of Vasil'evsky Island opposite, is a south-westerly mainland area roughly trapezoidal in shape, chiefly settled in the second half of the 18th century, and familiar to Sarah as Admiralty District, 4th Section. For her small corner she preferred the local name Malaya Kolomna, and indeed Admiralty 4th (popularly Kolomna) was renamed Kolomenskaya District later in the 19th century. It was and is bounded on the west by the main river and on the other sides by smaller waterways: the Moika on the north, the Krukov on the east and the Fontanka on the south.

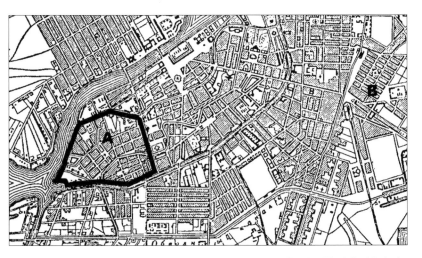

*Map of St Petersburg in 1849 (Tsylov), detail. The area outlined in black is Admiralty District, 4th Section, later Kolomenskaya District, with the site of Sarah's school (**A**) described in the text. NE is the Admiralty with its extensive squares. Running ESE from here is the famous Nevsky prospekt. E of this was the Community of Sisters of Charity (**B**) with the boarding school and the Grand Duchess Alexandra Nikolaevna Memorial Hospital (see Ch. 6). From **A** to **B** as the crow flies is about 5.25 km (3¼ miles).*

By the early 19th century Admiralty District boasted the most valuable properties in the city, including the famous Winter Palace, with grand building schemes. Although none of the other Admiralty sections were segregated socially and spatially in the way that might be expected, its 4th Section might be described as decidedly the least affluent quarter of an affluent district.[87] As late as 1869, between 26% and 45% of the houses in this Section (depending on the wards) were still wooden, compared to 5% or fewer in the adjacent area to the north-east. Industry was present too in Sarah's time, mainly shipbuilding, sugar refining and tobacco processing.[88] Only after the Mariinsky Theatre and the Conservatoire arrived in the 1860s did the area gradually become more 'desirable'.

Now we focus on the north-west corner of the trapezium. Here is a little canal called the Pryazhka, about a kilometre long, forming the vertical and curve of a J. The horizontal of the J is the Moika, and at its lower tip it meets the big river. Near the start of the curve is a bridge over the Pryazhka. It did not exist in Sarah's day, but the street leading to it and bisecting the Pryazhka Quay (naberezhnaya) did: now Decembrists Street (ulitsa Dekabristov), up to 1918 it was Officers Street (Ofitserskaya ulitsa). There, by the corner of this street and the quay, stood St Michael's Church House (dom tserkvi Sv. Mikhaila), home of Miss Kilham's Lancasterian School of Mutual Instruction for Poor Girls. The salient point is that this area is extremely close to the wide expanse of the Gulf of Finland and very exposed to the westerly gales characteristic of the autumn and early winter.

Sarah saw for herself what these gales could do on 7 November 1824. Reports followed of an earlier earthquake in Germany; it sounds rather like a tsunami. She told her stepmother about it at the first opportunity two days later. Here is a quite unfamiliar Sarah, her increasingly breathless excitement as she relives her experience casting grammar and punctuation to the winds as well:

> Between ten and eleven as we sat in school we observed the water running down the street in a small current, in the course of half an hour it increased so much as to form the whole street into a river, the wooden foot-roads began to give way and the bridges were loosened by the force of the water and all carried down the stream; people who were returning from market had no other alternative than that of trusting themselves to these floating ruins. One lady much mov'd our pity. First came in the current her cloak which made us fear a life had been lost; after that a droskie and horses, hardly manageable from the rapidity of the water, and last a lady and a little girl firmly holding each other and as pale as death, were standing on a broken bridge and steering *[travelling in their set course]* down the street at the will of our newly formed river.

...Just as the children were going to sit down to dinner I found we were in danger immediately afterward the water appear'd in one of the rooms; the little children I sent up stairs and all that could carry things away as I collected them together, the water increased rapidly and we continued walking about in it till it became too high to be manageable by that time we had removed all of consequence as well as laid up a store of provisions and when the children immediately afterwards chang'd their clothes and took wine to prevent any ill effects from the exposure and I have gratefully to acknowledge that we are all well and have not suffered from cold.[89]

'Her furniture was floating in her parlour', wrote Daniel Wheeler.[90] The water had risen to 9 feet in the street, she said, and to 3 or 7 feet in the school depending on the situation of the rooms. One end of the street was almost blocked by rafts, other streets by boats. 'Several whole villages have been swept away, inhabitants cattle and all. On Danl Wheeler's land have been thrown up many cows and there lie on it at present 15 dead bodies, one mother with a little girl under each arm is amongst the number'. She thought that at least a thousand people had died. (The official figure would be 15,000.) Workmen were helping to tidy up the school and it was hoped that by continual fires the rooms would be dry before long.[91]

People often try to spare older relatives the worst of bad news, and Sarah was franker when writing to her friend Ann Edmondson. All of them in the house and the courtyard were in 'the utmost confusion'. On the day of the flood she had been in water for three-quarters of an hour saving what she could – it was November, we recall, and the Russian winter had set in – and the next day she had had to wear wet shoes because she had lent her others to the children. The whole atmosphere was damp; that she had a bad cold was scarcely surprising. On Sunday she had not gone to Meeting. Instead she spent the time baking cakes for the children as no bread was on sale. Now she had had to send to Daniel Wheeler's to beg some bread.[92] She had no milk either, as all the milkman's cows had been drowned. Wheeler and his family, living on slightly higher ground, had escaped the flood. He managed to get through to check on her at the second attempt – all the city's wooden bridges were down – but meanwhile two of his children brought an item of news which adds to our understanding of her difficulties: she had had to make 'great exertions' on the children's behalf 'as all her day scholars were there when the flood came'.[93] So there had been about half as many children again to provide for, perhaps up to 40 in all.

Already in her letter to Ann and in the enduring crisis Sarah had exclaimed that she did not know what to do to help the poor around them. Three weeks later, calmer, she wrote again to Hannah. The death toll was now thought to be over 12,000, and she feared for people suffering greatly from their damp rooms. 'Ours are drying very nicely and I hope I feel thankful in saying the children have not suffer'd from cold, and mine is so far removed as to want no other care than the avoiding of night air'. Her main news, however, was of a poor relief fund in which John Venning was involved. 'He has kindly promised me 25 sheep skin coats tomorrow if I will send a cart for them which I shall of course do'. One's first impression is that these were for her boarding pupils, 25 being about the right number. Yet she immediately went on to say: 'we might make warm petticoats for the women and trowsers and shirts for the men',[94] so probably they were material for further processing (it depends on the meaning of 'coats') and this entailed a collective effort by the whole school.

Let us hear more from Sarah about the first four years of her school. On 29 December 1825 she reported that, as well as the ten free students, potentially 15, there were others, boarders and day pupils, who were maintained at their own expense. This is interesting because it suggests that the school was not, or no longer, perceived by the public as a place solely for destitute orphans. Attendances usually varied between 20 and 35, with more at times. Excluding certain pupils' own contributions, the school's annual income was 10,300 roubles: 8400 from the imperial budget for the upkeep of the building, and 1900 from the Imperial Philanthropic Society for the ten poor girls. It was superintended by Privy Councillor Stepan Semyonovich Dzhunkovsky,[95] Director of the Department of the State Economy and Public Buildings since 1811.

Now aged 63, Dzhunkovsky was a management expert with an interest in education and experience of England, for Catherine the Great had sent him abroad for advanced training in the physical sciences and agriculture, and on his return he was appointed English teacher to the three Grand Princes. Becoming Permanent Secretary of the Free Economic Society in 1803, he was to write widely on farm and household management. Thus he was well placed to initiate Sarah into the mysteries of running a Russian institution.[96] He was also a member of the governing body of James Heard's school, as we have seen, an activist in the Russian Bible Society,[97] and a committee member of the Society for the Care of Prisons.[98] He knew William Allen and one of his sons became very friendly with the Wheelers.

Sarah confirmed in her report that the school had been set up, and was conducted by her, on the principle of mutual instruction. Besides reading, writing and arithmetic, the girls were taught practical things – various manual skills befitting their poor station – to prepare them for working life. All the teachers apart from those of the three Rs also taught these crafts. (She did not record how many teachers there were or how they were paid.) The curriculum also included religious instruction in the Orthodox faith,[99] taught by a visiting priest. This was an abandonment

Sarah gives her Russian girls a needlework lesson.

of the Lancasterian principle of non-sectarianism, but for such schools to operate in Russia at all it was a sacrifice that had to be made. For Sarah, we suppose, it was made willingly. However history has judged the Emperor Alexander, we can take it from references in her letters that she revered him and respected his education minister Golitsyn, so that it was not only her duty but also her delight to run the school on the lines which they expected.

Yet from a letter home nearly two years later we surmise that the necessity of operating in this official faith context had become one of the most difficult parts of the job:

> The clergy feel their power tottering and are very jealous, so that it requires great prudence not to obstruct the course of instruction by ill-timed remarks, or attacks on their superstitions. I find it the best to direct to the sacrifice and example of the Saviour, regulating the conduct *[of the children]* according to the precepts of the Scriptures; and if they will be led to do this, we may leave all the rest, for the Holy Spirit will guide them into all truth.[100]

So what had been happening that provoked her opening comment here?

Just five weeks before Sarah filed her December 1825 report, her patron Alexander had died of typhoid, aged 47, at Taganrog in southern Russia.

Rumours persisted that he had wearied of his world of power and gone away incognito to spend the rest of his days as a hermit. His brother Constantine was unwilling to succeed him so he had secretly appointed their younger brother Nicholas his heir. For reasons which are unclear, however, Nicholas hesitated to claim the throne, causing confusion and restlessness, and by the time he did so he was faced with an uprising, the 'Decembrist Rebellion' of 14 December. Its upper-class leadership of mostly army officers, divided both in goals and tactics, sought either a constitutional monarchy or a republic. Nicholas had the backing of the Senate and his own Guards regiment, and after three fruitless attempts to persuade the 2000-plus rebels to surrender they were dispersed by cannon fire on the same day. Seven months later, after trials which they neither attended nor even knew about, five of the leaders were hanged; others were exiled to Siberia; others again, ordinary soldiers, were mercilessly flogged. This presaged the name by which Nicholas I would come to be known, Nikolai Palkin, which journalists of our own day would doubtless translate as Nick the Stick. But there was nothing funny about being beaten to death.

Nicholas was tall and handsome like his late brother, but whereas his brother was inconsistently harsh he was consistently so, to the point of sadism. The most notorious example of this came about much later, towards Christmas 1849. It sounds a bit like a re-run of the Decembrist affair, yet for a much milder offence. The young writer Fyodor Dostoevsky, secretly condemned to hard labour in Siberia for membership of the Petrashevsky Circle, a radical discussion group, but ignorant of the sentence, was taken from his cell early one morning with nineteen others. He had no idea why this was, or where they were going, until they reached a military parade ground with spectators, armed soldiers and a scaffold. For each man an official read out the sentence of death. It was not until the first three prisoners were tied to the stake and hooded, and the soldiers loaded and raised their guns, that the official suddenly announced that the Emperor had commuted the sentences to hard labour and exile. The execution ceremony had been a fake all along. Nicholas wanted to teach these young hotheads a lesson they would never forget.[101]

People were terrified of the Emperor. Wherever he went he was apt to jump on anybody, high or low, for breaking rules or neglecting standards. He reinforced direct control of government in 1826 by reorganizing his Chancellery into four (later six) 'departments'. The soon notorious 'Third Department' had charge of the political police. Censorship was another of his priorities; writers had to be very careful indeed. So he has gone down in history as the archetypal hard man among Russia's autocrats. Against this, a fairly recent study argues that he has been painted excessively dark, and finds evidence of a serious approach to administrative and social reform, though this was ultimately frustrated.[102] In the field of education we should note the advance in pupil numbers: from 62,000 in 1800 to some 250,000 in the 1830s and 450,000 in 1856.[103] Although in an estimated total population of 60 million this last figure points a long way to go, what Alexander had speeded up Nicholas had clearly continued over his thirty years at the helm.

In late December 1825 Sarah had smelled the whiff of rebellion but the rigours of the new regime still lay ahead. Very recent events had certainly been unsettling for her, but what about those over a wider timespan? We need to recapitulate. Paterson, Wheeler, Grellet, Allen and finally she herself had arrived in Russia over a decade, 1811-1821, that was highly propitious for their purposes. This coincided with the 'blessed' Emperor's growth of interest in religion, which reached its height in 1815 and was sustained thereafter, as the moral basis of reform. Symbolically, in October 1817 the Ministry of Public Education became the Ministry of Religious Affairs and Public Education (the 'Dual Ministry'), under Prince Golitsyn, for many years the lay head of the Orthodox Church and since 1813 founding President of the Russian Bible Society (RBS). Within the Ministry, the Department of Religious Affairs was headed by RBS secretary A.I. Turgenev and the Department of Public Education by the other RBS secretary V.M. Popov. For most of the decade the Emperor's Christianity was more mystical than Orthodox, and the Quakers Grellet and Allen gained a ready audience with him, his family and his Minister. Golitsyn took personal charge of their programme, assisted by Popov, and met them for silent prayer or discussion for two hours every other morning.[104]

Early in 1819, however, when Allen and Grellet undertook their abovementioned purge of the Lancasterian school reader and its replacement by a Biblical anthology, they unwittingly sowed the first seeds of disaster for their cause, in two ways. Firstly, in the wake of the French Revolution the Emperor and his government had long been suspicious of radical thinkers with 'Western' ideas, who now had evidently penetrated the military Lancasterian schools. The mutiny of the Semyonovsky Guards in October 1820 – though no connection has been proved – seemed to confirm it. This was part of a much wider picture: certain universities were purged, starting with Kazan' at the hands of M.L. Magnitsky in 1819, and secret societies and Masonic lodges were banned in 1822.

Secondly, parts of the Bible were now being made available to teach young people to read, on Alexander's own orders. In 1821 the RBS published the first complete edition of the New Testament in the Russian language. Although this had the backing of the political and much of the clerical leadership, there was no tradition in Russia for people to read the Scriptures. Worship was conducted in Church Slavonic, and many ordinary priests saw only harm in literacy. Who knew what wild, subversive notions folk might pick up by direct exposure to Holy Writ rather than through the Lord's official spokesmen and mediators? Another development was that the RBS roost came to be ruled by mystics with heterodox views who also held office in the Dual Ministry.[105] Many in the Orthodox Church became seriously alarmed. With the Emperor away, supporters of the Bible Society and the schools began to feel embattled. Sarah may not have experienced this directly but was certainly aware of it through her membership of the committee managing James Heard's new school.

Eventually Alexander was himself persuaded that his lofty plans to regenerate the nation had backfired. In May 1824 Golitsyn was sacked and the Dual Ministry was abolished. The presidency of the RBS went to a leading Orthodox cleric, Metropolitan (chief archbishop) Serafim of St Petersburg, who sought its downfall. The new Minister of Education was A.S. Shishkov, a retired admiral with arch-conservative views who saw the RBS as a gang of British crusaders for Protestantism. In its next report, the parent society in London referred with exquisite tact to 'difficulties which have arisen',[106] while the odious Magnitsky, appointed six years earlier to the new Committee for the Establishment of Schools of Mutual Instruction and now with his old boss Golitsyn safely out of the way, denounced the Lancasterian system as 'nothing other than propaganda of the Quaker sect'.[107] The RBS would be all but abolished in 1826. The last straw was probably its British links at a time of new Russian aspirations in the Balkans, entailing an anti-British change in foreign policy.[108]

In such a different climate Sarah would have been less than human not to have wondered about her own future and that of her school. The new Emperor regarded himself as God's Field-Marshal and followed priorities which in 1832 would be epitomized by S.S. Uvarov as the principles of 'autocracy, Orthodoxy and [Russian] nationality' (or national identity). Belief in these must imbue education. Uvarov was promoted to Minister of Education in 1833[109] and Nicholas made these watchwords his own. It is impossible to imagine him hob-nobbing with Quakers as his predecessor had done, and we have found no record of Sarah having an audience with him as she had once had with Alexander. So, we suppose, she continued in her quiet, efficient way, impressing her government masters with her financial management skills[110] and taking care to hold her counsel on religious matters. Her strategy and tactics paid off. As we shall see, after a lengthy visit to England she was not only to get her old job back but also to receive further commissions.

Joining the Independents

Meanwhile, however, let us consider Sarah's doings out of school in the second half of her first Russian decade. During 1825 things continued much as before. She attended Meeting at Daniel Wheeler's, who included her as one of his 'own dear family' when imparting blessings at the close of a letter to George Edmondson.[111] He reported her to be in good health when writing later in the year to George, who had returned with his family to Sheffield to stay with his Singleton in-laws in Fargate.[112] About May 1826, however, she abruptly stopped coming to Meeting. In July Daniel notified this to the Overseers of Sheffield Meeting, enclosing a copy of her letter of resignation, which has not survived. He had immediately called on her, but she had gone to Kronstadt (until the 1880s the capital's deep-water port) 'with a party of her newly acquired associates' to see some of them off to England. The next day she was at home and he had hoped for an explanation, but she was more obstinate than candid. We have already noticed how resolute she could be. Sarah did, however, confirm that she 'had no wish to renounce Friends',[113] and Daniel told George Edmondson three months later that they were still on friendly terms.[114] Even so, the once close relationship between her and the Wheelers is bound to have become rather tense.

We might have expected Sarah Kilham to return to the church of her father, but Methodist preaching at St Petersburg began under the auspices of the American Methodist Episcopal Church only in 1881 or 1882, in Swedish and later Finnish; in 1907 in Russian; and in 1908 in English.[115] Sarah had defected to what was commonly known as Richard Knill's chapel, or as Daniel Wheeler explained in his letter to the Sheffield Overseers, 'a congregation of the Scotch Independents'. Both terms are a little misleading, inasmuch as they were not all Scots and, as previously mentioned, they were sharing the established chapel of the German Moravians at this stage of their history. Sarah had been acquainted with the minister for about five years through her membership of the governing body of his School for Poor Foreign Children, but neither of them refers to the other until around this time. We too met Richard Knill earlier and a closer acquaintance is due.

Knill's unusual name stems from a Herefordshire hamlet almost literally on the Welsh border, although he himself was a native of Braunton in North Devon. He had been a missionary in India and needed a change of climate. His needs were met drastically when he arrived in St Petersburg in December 1821. Originally appointed to the London Missionary Society's Selenginsk station south of Lake Baikal in Siberia, he instead took charge of a 40-member congregation established in the capital on the initiative of John Paterson.[116] After a year he had doubled the membership and trebled the congregation.[117] Soon he informed headquarters that his mission ought to have its own place of worship, and a subscription was opened in London. He had also started a Tuesday evening meeting for young people, with sixteen members aged from 9 to 15:

'they... often make very judicious remarks on the books which they read, and the things which they see and hear'.[118] He also set up three prayer meetings in different parts of the city so that his members could get to them more easily.[119]

Shortly afterwards Knill married Sarah Nottman, at just 27 eight years his junior. Born in St Petersburg, she was the daughter of a Newcastle-on-Tyne Quaker who had set up tanneries in various parts of the Russian Empire.[120] The ceremony was conducted at what he called the English Factory Chapel, better known as the English Church, by the Rev Edward Law, the (Anglican) Chaplain, followed by a wedding breakfast at Dr Paterson's. The English Church, opened on the south bank of the Neva in 1754, was home to a well-heeled expatriate congregation who tended to look down their noses at nonconformists.[121] When, after a very awkward start, Richard Knill and Edward Law became good colleagues and cooperated in educational work, some of Law's members were evidently none too pleased.[122]

What were the reasons for Sarah's change of allegiance? According to Daniel Wheeler she had largely lost her Quaker convictions. 'I am not at all surprised by it', he commented to George Edmondson, 'from a belief that the principles of Friends were lightly esteemed by her'; and to the Overseers he wrote, 'I have long looked upon her as only a nominal member of our society'.[123] This again begs reflections why. Sarah did in fact give a reason in the 1827 letter to her uncle in Epworth, going on to pay tribute to Richard Knill:

> My beloved mother will probably have told you I am no longer united to the religious society of which she is a member. I trust in seeking the *instruction* I needed, I have been following the leadings of Providence... The minister of the chapel which I attend... is an eminently pious man, earnest, clear, and affectionate in his addresses to the people – a pastor who enters into their joys and sorrows, and to whom they may look for example and counsel.[124]

Daniel Wheeler was a man of the utmost integrity but comes across as dour and severe. Sarah was not the self-contained loner that another person in such a self-imposed, isolated situation might have been. Teacher and pastor, she herself needed pastoring and teaching, but in Daniel she found neither the former, because of his personality, nor the latter, because of his role-perception. Referring to the Society of Friends, he continued to the Overseers: 'it is a lamentable reflection that any of its members should be so destitute as to expect to derive *Spiritual advantage* from the ministry of any *man*'.[125]

As Quakers, both Daniel and Sarah were the victims of circumstance too. Six months later we find him writing to the Sheffield Friends:

Our little meeting now reduced to only six members of Society, which are those of my own family and three of these being in the minority, we have of late been brought more closely into the solid consideration of our humiliating and stripped condition.[126]

It can be hard to abandon a small, familiar group and still harder to accept being abandoned.

Here the Wheelers' part in Sarah's story has been played out, but such pioneers deserve at least a short sketch of the rest of their own lives. Daniel resigned his post in 1832 and his son William took it over. He returned to England to await the Lord's will. His wife Jane opted to stay in Russia with the children, but before the year was out she was dead. This brought Daniel back briefly, then he embarked on a four-year missionary journey to the South Seas with his son Charles. Meanwhile William handed his work over to Daniel junior, but his plans to enter a partnership in Finland's first cotton mill were thwarted by his death from consumption in 1836. The story of the young Wheelers becomes sadder and sadder. Lively, temperamental Jenny died in 1837, aged just 21, to be mourned by her father on his last Russian visit. Within eleven years, back in England, all her other brothers had followed her. Their father's own pilgrimage ended in New York on 13 June 1840.[127]

Let us return to 1827 and to Sarah. She had been a loyal member of the 'little meeting' for nearly six years, crossing the city on first-days from west to east, over the Neva and back again. There was no Okhta Bridge in those times, and when ferries could not operate during the freeze and the thaw, or the ice was unsafe, the river was impassable. Had the group remained larger, with others of Sarah's age, the outcome might have been different. For there was surely a further reason for her leaving, not stated by anyone but implicit in Daniel Wheeler's slightly bitter remark about her going off with her 'newly acquired associates' to Kronstadt:[128] when off duty she had felt lonely in this foreign city and had been looking for people of a similar background and age with whom she could share her free time. She was now 38. Whether she yet had a particular man in her sights one may doubt, but she was always very reticent about her private life, as we shall see, and so the possibility cannot be entirely ruled out.

There was, however, another man thanks to whom we have a few sidelights on Sarah Kilham's social activities: Richard Knill. The first Kilham reference in his manuscript journal is in fact to Hannah, back from her first missionary journey to the Gambia and Sierra Leone (October 1823 to August 1824) and now based mainly in London. One of her current causes was the poverty in the slums of Spitalfields where the silk weavers were suffering from foreign competition and the recent introduction of power looms. She advocated, among other things, the setting up of infant schools there.[129] Richard must have known of her either through missionary circles or through Sarah on his school committee, perhaps both. In an entry for 17 November 1825 he mentions a plan for his niece Eliza 'to undertake the charge of a school at St Giles under the auspices of good Mrs Kilham'.[130] The plan worked: a few months later Eliza was 'employed as teacher of a Lancasterian school for poor Irish girls in St Giles – where she has about 120 fine young girls... if I had not been what I am [a LMS missionary with Lancasterian contacts] it is not likely she would be employed as she is'. His nephew was to run a Lancasterian school in Kidderminster.[131]

School business was quite possibly the occasion for the first meeting with Sarah Kilham that Richard Knill recorded in his journal for 26 March 1826: 'Called on Miss Kilham and Mr Heard'. Then he 'took tea' with her on 7 May, just about the time when she stopped attending the Friends' Meeting. This was almost certainly to discuss her becoming a member of his congregation, for on 22 August he wrote: 'Administered the Lord's Supper. Miss Kilham [and two others] sat down with us for the first time'. One of the others was Betsy Gray, probably related to the master of the boys' division of his School for Poor Foreign Children. More social events followed: Sarah came to breakfast on 30 September, and on 7 October he entered: 'Dined with the Gillibrands at Miss Kilham's'. Richard visited her again in November.[132]

William Clarke Gellibrand (1791-1884) – the correct spelling – and his first wife Elizabeth became close friends of Sarah's. He was one of the most eminent members of her expatriate circle. Born at Ringwood, Hants, the elder son of a dissenting minister – who was something of a black sheep but ended up as a leading citizen of Hobart, Tasmania – he went to Russia in 1815 to work for his merchant relatives the Morgans in Moscow. Seven years later he entered into partnership with J.G. Hubbard & Co., also linked to his extended family by marriage; John Hubbard's middle name was Gellibrand. The firm imported lead and tin from England and exported tallow, hemp, flax and grain. In the 1840s they expanded their activities into spinning at St Petersburg and timber near Archangel.[133]

Daniel Wheeler had acidly referred to Sarah's new involvement in the social life of Richard's congregation, and we hear of her sharing in more formal activities too. In January 1827 she paid her annual dues of 20 roubles. These varied among the members, five paying 25 and one 100. If such dues were income-related, Sarah must have counted as fairly well off.[134] She also took her part in charitable giving – 8 roubles for shirts for James Lyon, an impoverished young student going to England to further his education – and proposed raising a collection to pay the tavern bill of a Mr Groves and his family, missionaries on their way through St

Petersburg to Persia. On New Year's Eve 1828 Richard treated his journal to a spiritual stock-taking of his congregation, all done very positively with no harsh words. He drew up a long list of blessings, and then went on to consider his people's virtues: 'Sarah Kilham is worthy to be held up as an example, for humility, diligence, self-denial, zeal &c... Blessed be God for such a Flock'.[135]

Tracts and Testaments

A new interest which Sarah developed at this time and which became very important to her was voluntary work for the Bible Societies. As a missionary himself Richard Knill made sure that his congregation knew about it and encouraged them to support it. We may well wonder, however, how this was still possible, given the hostility to the Russian Bible Society that had come to a head in 1824. What had happened since? Clutching at a straw, the British and Foreign Bible Society informed its members in 1826 that the new Emperor had renewed his subscription to the RBS.[136] This did not stop him suspending the RBS that August. There was a minor consolation: he expressly permitted the sale of existing stocks of the Scriptures in Russian and the other languages of the Empire. Reporting this, John Paterson, who had been winding up the BFBS's Russian business, found it possible to request some German Testaments for the colonists in the south, and 1000 copies were sent.[137] This heralded not exactly a new dawn but certainly a break in the encircling gloom: in 1828 Nicholas I sanctioned the formation of a Protestant Bible Society in Russia, headed by former ambassador to London Prince Lieven. The new society had 20,000 copies of the Scriptures ready for distribution and 13,000 roubles in the bank.[138]

Richard Knill set up a fund for Finnish bibles, to be bought at 2 roubles apiece and sold to needy Finns (Finland was under Russian rule at this time). He listed some three dozen contributors, of whom 27 had English names, four German and three Russian. 'Miss Kilham' gave a respectable 25 roubles and a certain 'Mr Billar' – of whom more later – a very generous 70 roubles; subsequently he donated 25 roubles towards fitting up a missionary ship. In 1829 'dear Miss Kilham' began to play her part along with Richard in obtaining and disposing of tracts in Russian and prayer books in Finnish, the latter also involving Pastor Mortimer, who was the Moravian minister and hence the British congregation's landlord.[139] Tracts meant contact with the Tract Society in London, but the records are too sketchy to be confident about the details of that operation at this stage.

As for the Scriptures, a 'St Petersburg correspondent' informed the BFBS in time for the 1830 *Report* that 700 more copies, mainly of Russian Testaments, had been drawn from the warehouses and distributed, bringing the total (dispensed by him, presumably) to 2500, almost all sold at a reduced price. A further 7000 Testaments in German, French and Russian had been placed at his disposal, the last batch of these containing 2000 copies in Russian.[140] This news conveys an odd mixture of caution and temerity. The correspondent whose name was cautiously withheld was Richard Knill – he had made a similar request to the BFSS for anonymity at a difficult time for his school a few years earlier[141] – though in 1832 the BFBS would let the cat out of the bag.[142]

The temerity revolves round the origin of the 7000 Testaments. The Russian ones could not have come from the new Protestant Bible Society, as that body did not publish in Russian. If any remained from the unsold stock of the old RBS it was illegal to cut the price.[143] If they were newly supplied directly or indirectly from the BFBS in England, particularly the Russian ones, this was a somewhat risky infringement of the 1826 decree, certainly in the spirit if not in the letter. Much the same could be said about the Russian-language tracts. In the winter of 1829/30 two members of Knill's congregation were in fact arrested for distributing tracts and Testaments; one was expelled and the other imprisoned.[144] The situation would, however, become easier.

Meanwhile, discretion was of the essence. There is a fascinating note at the end of the BFBS *Report* for 1830: 'To a zealous female of the Society of Friends, in Petersburgh [sic], 210 copies of the Scriptures in German, French and English have been granted'.[145] The pseudonym 'a zealous female' would suit Sarah Kilham very well. But it raises a question. The problem is, of course, that she had stopped being a Quaker all of four years before. Either some BFBS editor was drawing false inferences from associations with the Kilham name, or this person really was a Quaker. Who else could it have been?

There were very few candidates. One possibility was Daniel Wheeler's elder daughter Sarah, aged 23 in 1830, probably the 'pious young Quakeress' actually named as 'Miss Wheeler' who would be giving help to Richard Knill a year later.[146] But she was shy, while her much more outgoing sister Jenny was only 15 at the time. Moreover, distributing Scriptures was not a normal activity for the Wheelers. Such speculations were, however, cut short when two letters from Sarah Kilham to the BFBS written in summer 1830 and early in 1831 came to light. The first alluded to '60 Bibles & 150 Testaments... kindly sent to a few individuals in Petersburg last summer' – she asked for this to be kept out of the *Report* but perhaps she missed the deadline – and the second referred to 'a liberal grant for the use of foreigners in Russia' made to her by the Society eighteen months earlier.[147] We conclude that this instance of female zeal was not Quakerly but it was surely Kilhamite.

We must not read too much into the fact that Richard Knill began in October 1829 to refer to Sarah as 'dear Miss Kilham'. Harvey Pitcher comments that it was always a strong part of the British Chapel's appeal for its congregation to think of themselves as a beleaguered minority,[148] and such modes of address were an outward form of the spiritual glue binding them together. The same phenomenon occurs on a much larger scale among the Quakers, historically a prime example of a persecuted group. The usage became customary, so much so that when a highly exasperated Daniel Wheeler complained about what he saw as William Allen's thoughtless actions he still called him 'dear William Allen'.[149] It might also be projected on to kindred spirits outside the group, as when Allen wrote to Vasily Popov referring to Alexander as 'the dear Emperor'.[150] Richard Knill and Sarah Kilham had become good friends in a common cause. If anything is mildly surprising, it is that it took Richard over three years to start using the term, a reaction perhaps to natural reticence on Sarah's part.

Late in 1829 Richard saw S.S. Dzhunkovsky, whose son Alexander had been entrusted to William Allen in March 1825 to further his education in England and on returning to Russia over three years later had reported to Allen that Sarah's school was going on prosperously and increasing rapidly.[151] Dzhunkovsky gave Richard some hot news of Sarah which sent him off straightway to find her. Probably she had just informed her employers that she was seeking leave of absence for a protracted period. She had people to see and business to attend to back in England. On 13 May 1830 it was her turn, with another friend, Miss Musgrave, to be accompanied to Kronstadt by Richard. As was usual on such occasions, they took letters and papers from him to be forwarded to such bodies as the Bible Society, the Tract Society and the *Evangelical Magazine*.[152] He waved them off as they set sail on the *Halcyon*, a name fit to propitiate stormy seas (it means the kingfisher, once believed to charm the wind and the waves so as to incubate its eggs on the water's surface). It would be nearly a year before they met again.

Notes and References

1   FHL: Port 41/156, GE to John Edmondson, 7 Sep 1820. In references to their correspondence the various protagonists are cited thus: GE, George Edmondson; DW, Daniel Wheeler; JV, John Venning; WA, William Allen. 'Lancastrian' is an alternative spelling.

2   SA: QR 64, Balby Monthly Meeting, Register of Removals 1812-1827, pp 64-5. While the Balby minute was signed 'the 13th day of the 9th Month 1820', George's letter was actually dated '9 mo 7/19 1820'. Our Quaker correspondents in Russia expose their modern readers to a double danger of

dating. At this time Russia still employed the Julian (Old Style) Calendar; twelve days were added for the equivalent date in the Gregorian (New Style) Calendar used in England. Sometimes people writing from St Petersburg gave both dates, as here, or added O.S. We shall keep to their dates as given, assuming them to be Old Style – as they usually were – when not specified, but converting them to abbreviated non-Quaker usage; thus '9 mo 7' or '7th of 9th mo' becomes 7 Sep.

3   FHL: Temp Mss 366/I/8/1, 'Minutes of Friends Constituting the Meeting at Ochta near Petersburgh'; letter referring to 'S.K.' in *Memoirs of the Life and Gospel Labours of the Late Daniel Wheeler* (London, 1842), p 88 (henceforth *Wheeler*).

4   Cited in Greenwood, 2, p 144; no source stated.

5   Hollingsworth, pp 66-8.

6   Greenwood, 2, p 144; no source stated but referring evidently to an undated letter of 1821 (FHL: Temp Mss 366/I/38, WA to DW). The letter must have been written early in the year before Allen had heard about Walter Venning's death.

7   Greenwood, 2, pp 122-3; on his missing them, letter of March 1819 quoted in F. Wilson, *Muscovy: Russia through Foreign Eyes, 1553-1900* (London, 1970), p 206.

8   FHL: Port 41/157, GE to John Edmondson, 5 Dec 1820.

9   FHL: Temp Mss 366/I/38, WA to DW, 1821 (no full date).

10 DW to David Mallinson, Feb 1820, quoted in Wilson, p 203. Sarah was there through the following winter.

11 FHL: Port 41/161, GE to Agnes Edmondson, 6 Mar 1821.

12 J. Muckle, *The Russian Language in Britain: A Historical Study of Learners and Teachers* (Ilkeston, 2008), pp 22, 24-7.

13 Ibid., pp 19-22.

14 *Allen*, 2, pp 211-12.

15 *Report of the BFSS*, 16 (1821), p 18.

16 RGIA (Russian State Historical Archive, St Petersburg): f. 1409, op. 2, d. 4576 (hereafter on pattern 1409/2/4576), 'Ob uchilishche anglichanki Sarry Kalgam dlya bednykh detei zhenskogo pola' (On the Englishwoman Sarah Kilham's school for poor female children), 29 December 1825, f lv (hereafter 'Ob uchilishche anglichanki'). I am most grateful to Dr Julia Mahnke-Devlin for supplying me with extracts from her thesis 'Briten in St Petersburg und Moskau im 19. Jahrhundert' (PhD, Ludwig-Maximilians-Universität München, 2002) and copies of her research notes, and for tracking down this reference in the first place. The thesis has since been published as *Britische Migration nach Russland im 19. Jahrhundert* (Wiesbaden, 2005), here p 220. Greenwood's founding date of 1822 (2, p 144) is incorrect.

17 Zacek, p 352, apparently based on *Allen*, 1, p 463.

18 'Ob uchilishche po metode vzaimnogo obucheniya dlya devits', *Sorevonovatel' prosveshcheniya i blagotvoreniya*, pt 23 (1823), pp 216-18, cited in W. Rosslyn, 'Women with a Mission: British Female Evangelicals in the Russian Empire in the Early Nineteenth Century', in W. Rosslyn and A. Tosi, ed., *Women in Russian Culture and Society, 1700-1825* (Basingstoke and New York, 2007), p 223.

19 Ibid., presumably from the same source.
20 FHL: Temp Mss 366/I/41, WA to DW, 6 Mar 1822.
21 Hollingworth, p 66; Zacek, p 350.
22 *Allen*, 2, p 220.
23 C.M. Birrell, *The Life of the Rev. Richard Knill, of St Petersburgh*, 3rd edn (London, 1860), p 96.
24 Ibid.; School of Oriental and African Studies (SOAS), University of London: Council for World Mission/London Missionary Society/Europe, Russia/Incoming Correspondence, Box 1, Folder 5, Jacket A (hereafter on pattern CWM, Russia, In. Corr., 1/5/A), Richard Knill (RK) to W.A. Hankey, 2 Oct 1821; Russia/Journals/Box 1, Journal of Richard Knill, 1819-1831 (hereafter CWM, Russia, RK's Journal), 29 Oct 1821, p 4. I am especially grateful to James Muckle for alerting me years ago to the existence of Knill's manuscript Journal.
25 Wardle and Pratt's *Directory of Sheffield 1816-17*, Tables, p 8.
26 Derived from rates for 2007 at www.measuringworth.com, accessed in 2008.
27 *Report of the BFSS*, 18 (1823), p 98; *Allen*, 2, pp 233-4.
28 CWM, Russia, In. Corr., 1/6/A, RK to D. Bogue, 3 Aug 1823.
29 *Report of the BFSS*, 18 (1823), p 100.
30 CWM, Russia, In. Corr., 1/6/A, RK to D. Bogue, 3 Aug 1823.
31 GARF (Main Archive of the Russian Federation, Moscow): 109/3/2654, *Quatrième rapport de l'école établie en faveur des enfans* [sic] *pauvres parmi les étrangers qui se trouvent à St Pétersbourg pour 1826* (St Petersburg, 1826); Mahnke-Devlin, p 222.
32 Zacek, p 354.
33 *Allen*, 2, p 230.
34 FHL: Gibson IV/109, HK to Mrs Thomas Thompson, 6 Sept 1825 (year indistinct but postmark 1825); CWM, Russia, RK's Journal, pp 88-9 (recording death of Mr [William] Spurr on 1 Aug 1824 aged 26).
35 *Allen*, 2, p 233.
36 T.S. Henderson, *Memorials of John Venning, Esq.* (London, 1862), pp 232-3.
37 FHL: Temp Mss 366/I/41, WA to DW, 6 Mar 1822.
38 *Report of the BFSS*, 17 (1822), p 30.
39 Zacek, p 354.
40 *Report of the BFSS*, 18 (1823), p 98.
41 Henderson, p 233; Zacek, p 355. Hollingsworth (p 69) is incorrect on two points: the school was authorized, not opened, in 1822, and the initial grant of 5000 roubles was for the school for poor foreign children, not this one.
42 *Report of the BFSS*, 18 (1823), p 98. Henderson (p 233) gives the initial enrolment as 62.
43 Zacek, p 354.
44 *Report of the BFSS*, 19 (1824), p 30.
45 Ibid., 18 (1823), p 29.
46 *Allen*, 2, p 338.
47 FHL: Temp Mss 4/3, JV to WA, 3 Sep 1823.
48 Henderson, p 233.
49 Ibid. Correct title: Curator of the St Petersburg Educational District.
50 Hollingsworth, p 66; Zacek, p 350.

51 S.B. Paina, 'Vol'noe obshchestvo uchrezhdeniya uchilishch vzaimnogo obucheniya (1818-1825 gg.). II. Deyatel'nost' obshchestva', *NIPN*, 12 (1968), p 107.

52 Ibid., p 108; Paina (1973), p 13.

53 S.B. Paina, 'Vol'noe obshchestvo uchrezhdeniya uchilishch vzaimnogo obucheniya (1818-1825 gg.). I. Organizatsiya, sostav i zadachi obshchestva', *NIPN*, 10 (1967), p 125; Paina (1968), p 108. But according to Hollingsworth (p 64) the Free Society had three schools in St Petersburg and the first closed in 1827.

54 A.M. Martin, *Romantics, Reformers, Reactionaries* (DeKalb, IL, 1997), pp 161, 164.

55 W. Rosslyn, 'Benevolent Ladies and their Exertions for the Good of Humankind: V.A. Repnina, S.S. Meshcherskaia, and the Origins of Female Philanthropy in Early Nineteenth-Century Russia', *Slavonic and East European Review*, 84 (2006), pp 52-82.

56 Ibid., p 67.

57 I.T. Osinin, ed, 'Zapiski kvakera o prebyvanii v Rossii', *Russkaya starina*, 9 (1874), pp 3-4 (quotation retranslated); this source was more accessible to me than B. Seebohm, ed., *Memoirs of the Life and Gospel Labours of Stephen Grellet* (London and Bradford, 1860).

58 Rosslyn, 'Benevolent Ladies', pp 67-9, 73-5.

59 Ibid., pp 69-70.

60 *Allen*, 1, p 424.

61 Ibid., p 448.

62 Ibid., p 450; 2, pp 22, 36.

63 e.g. *Allen*, 2, pp 209, 220, 222, 353.

64 So it appears from Henderson, p 232.

65 Ibid., p 236.

66 *Allen*, 2, p 234.

67 Ibid., p 265.

68 Quotation from *Report of the BFSS*, 19 (1824) p 30; see also 18 (1823), pp 29, 98; 19 (1824), p 106; 22 (1827), p 11; 23 (1828), p 8; 25 (1830), p 11; and *Brief Account* (bound in with 1830 *Report*), p 3. Although the last-named mentions a school for girls, the context of preceding and following annual reports suggests that the provision for poor foreign children is meant.

69 FHL: Port 41/165, GE to Agnes Edmondson, 1/13 Jan 1824; our emphasis.

70 Hollingsworth, p 70.

71 Henderson, p 229, also highlights this purpose.

72 SK [to Simon Kilham junior], 6 Sept 1827, in 'Letter from Miss Kilham, Daughter of the Late Rev. A. Kilham, to her Uncle', *New Methodist* [MNC] *Magazine and Evangelical Repository*, 33 (1830), p 278 (hereafter SK, *NMM*, 33 (1830)).

73 SK to Simon Kilham junior, 24 Oct 1831, in 'Religious Intelligence: Letter of Miss Kilham, of Russia', *NMM*, 35 (1832), p 82 (hereafter SK, *NMM*, 35 (1832)).

74 FHL: Gibson IV/109, HK to Mrs Thomas Thompson, 6 Sept 1825.

75 B. Forsythe, articles on the Vennings, *Dictionary of National Biography*, 56 (Oxford, 2004), pp 265-6 and 267-8; Rosslyn, 'Benevolent Ladies', pp 73-4.

76 Henderson, p 170.

77 Comment about wheels from J.H. Bater, *St Petersburg: Industrialisation and Change* (London, 1976), p 64.

78 Henderson, p 223.

79 Ibid., pp 205-6, 216.

80 Ibid., pp 223-4.

81 Ibid., p 230.

82 Ibid., p 231.

83 Sarah Biller (hereafter SB) to JV, 18 Oct 1841, in Henderson, p 232; *Gorodskoi ukazatel' ili adresnaya kniga... na 1850 god* (St Petersburg, 1849), p 451.

84 'Ob uchilishche po metode', cited in Rosslyn, 'Women with a Mission', p 233.

85 SK, *NMM*, 33 (1830), p 278.

86 Maps of St Petersburg in 1799 and 1849 are in E. Lopatina, *Leningrad* (Moscow, 1959), facing pp 48, 49.

87 Based on Bater, pp 35, 38, 78.

88 Ibid., pp 59, 156.

89 FHL: Temp Mss 407/6, SK to HK, 9/21 Nov 1824 (copied extract).

90 *Wheeler*, p 113, citing DW to John Hipsley, 11 Nov 1824 O.S.

91 FHL: Temp Mss 407/6, SK to HK, 9/21 Nov 1824.

92 FHL: Port D/65, SK to Ann Edmondson, undated (10 Nov?).

93 FHL: Port 41/179 and 181, DW to GE, both 10 Nov 1824; *Wheeler*, pp 111, 113.

94 FHL: Temp Mss 407/6, SK to HK, 30 Nov 1824.

95 'Ob uchilishche anglichanki', ff 1v-3; also in Mahnke-Devlin (2005), pp 220-1.

96 F.A. Brokgauz and I.A. Efron, *Novyi entsiklopedicheskii slovar'*, 16 (St Petersburg, n.d.), cols 103-4; *Alfavitnyi ukazatel' imën russkikh deyatelei dlya Russkogo biograficheskogo slovarya*, reprint of 1887-88 edn (Nendeln, 1976), p 199.

97 Zacek, p 355.

98 Rosslyn, 'Benevolent Ladies', p 74.

99 'Ob uchilishche anglichanki', ff 1-2v; Mahnke-Devlin (2005), p 220.

100 SK, *NMM*, 33 (1830), p 278.

101 H. Troyat, *Firebrand: The Life of Dostoevsky* (London and Toronto, 1946), pp 127-34.

102 D. Saunders, *Russia in the Age of Reaction and Reform 1801-1881* (London and New York, 1992), pp 119-44.

103 Ibid., p 152.

104 Thus Grellet in Osinin, ed., pp 3, 9.

105 Martin, pp 186, 189-90.

106 *Report of the British and Foreign Bible Society* (henceforth *BFBS*), 21 (1825), p xxxiv (distinguished from BFSS reports by roman pagination).

107 Quoted in Zacek, p 366.

108 S.B. Okun', *Ocherki istorii SSSR. Konets XVIII – pervaya chetvert' XIX veka* (Leningrad, 1956), p 302.
109 Sanders, p 117.
110 Henderson, p 230, gives grounds for this conjecture.
111 FHL: Port 41/183, DW to GE, 27 Jan 1825.
112 FHL: Port 41/184, DW to GE, 12 Oct 1825.
113 FHL: Temp Mss 407/10, DW to Overseers of Sheffield Meeting.
114 FHL: Port 41/185, DW to GE, 13 Oct 1826.
115 J. Dunstan, 'George A. Simons and the Khristianski Pobornik', *Methodist History*, 19 (1980), pp 23-6, 32.
116 *Report of the London Missionary Society [LMS]*, 27 (1821), p 68; Pitcher, pp 8-9.
117 CWM, Russia, RK's Journal, p 5.
118 *Report of the LMS*, 29 (1823), pp 82-3.
119 Ibid., 30 (1824), p 93.
120 Birrell, p 100.
121 Pitcher, p 5; CWM, Russia, In. Corr., 1/6/C, RK to W.A. Hankey, 24 Jan 1824; RK's Journal, pp 32, 79.
122 CWM, Russia, In. Corr., 1/6/C, RK to G. Burder, 22 Jan 1824 and W.A. Hankey, 4 May 1824; RK's Journal, pp 64-5, 84.
123 FHL: Port 41/185, DW to GE, 13 Oct 1826; Temp Mss 407/10, DW to Overseers of Sheffield Meeting, 10 July 1826.
124 SK, *NMM*, 33 (1830), p 278; our emphasis.
125 FHL: Temp Mss 407/10, DW to Overseers, 10 July 1826; his emphasis.
126 FHL: Temp Mss 366/I/61, DW to Balby Monthly Meeting, 26 Jan 1827.
127 Scott, pp 77-9, 80-1; Greenwood, 2, pp 138, 140, 145.
128 FHL: Temp Mss 407/10, DW to Overseers, 10 July 1826.
129 Dickson, pp 191, 197, 199-200.
130 CWM, Russia, RK's Journal, p 145.
131 CWM, Russia, In. Corr., 2/1/C, RK to W.A. Hankey, 2/14 Apr and 10 June 1826. Although St Giles Cripplegate is fairly close to Spitalfields, the parish is more likely to be the more distant St Giles-in-the-Fields, notorious for its slum known *inter alia* as 'Little Dublin' which was partly cleared to build New Oxford Street in the mid-1840s (P. Ackroyd, *London: The Biography* (London, 2000), pp 137-42).
132 CWM, Russia, RK's Journal, pp 161, 168, 177, 183, 184, 189.
133 J. Livingston, *Gellibrands* ([Belvedere], 2005), pp 51, 53-4; copy in Leeds Russian Archive (LRA): Ms 1110/6.
134 CWM, Russia, RK's Journal, p 195.
135 Ibid., pp 188, 230, 235.
136 *Report of the BFBS*, 22 (1826), p xxxii.
137 Ibid., 23 (1827), p xl.
138 Ibid., 24 (1828), p l.
139 CWM, Russia, RK's Journal, pp 230, 263, 264, 267, 269.
140 *Report of the BFBS*, 26 (1830), p xl.
141 CWM, Russia, In. Corr., 2/1/A, RK to Hankey, 3/15 Feb 1826.
142 *Report of the BFBS*, 28 (1832), p xlvi.
143 Ibid., 23 (1827), p xl; 29 (1833), p xlvi.

144 Pitcher, pp 11-12.
145 *Report of the BFBS*, 30 (1826), p xli.
146 CWM, Russia, In. Corr., 2/4/A, RK to John Arundell, 18/30 Sept 1831.
147 Cambridge University Library, Bible Society Library: BSA/D1/2/31, SK to Josiah Foster, 3 July 1830; BSA/D1/2/33, SK to John Jackson, 8 Jan 1831.
148 Pitcher, p 9.
149 Greenwood, 2, p 144.
150 *Allen*, 2 , pp 181, 182.
151 Ibid., 2, pp 395-6 and 3, p 6 (A. Dzhunkovsky to WA, 15/27 Sept 1828).
152 CWM, Russia, RK's Journal, pp 270, 278.

4. FAMILY AFFAIRS AND BIBLE BUSINESS

SARAH'S ENGLISH INTERLUDE

Farewell to Hannah

THE *HALCYON* lived up to its name and Sarah arrived safely. The England awaiting her had seen few drastic changes in her absence. The 1820s were heralded by the accession of George IV and the 1830s by his death. The enclosure movement had continued and people moved to the towns. The post-war depression brought factory closures and unemployment, and pauperism increased. In Sarah's nonconformist milieu, however, towards the end of the decade, men improved their position when laws preventing them from holding public office were repealed. She must have been too preoccupied with personal concerns to take much notice of these matters. Later, recalling her stay, she wrote: 'Whilst memory holds her seat, my heart must feel the mercy and blessing of that visit to England, fraught, however, with responsibilities'.[1] These duties related to her stepmother, her late father and the Bible Society, but she also made time to visit friends and relations.

Hannah Kilham had previously tried to draw Sarah away from the school in St Petersburg, perhaps to apply her educational talents in Africa or elsewhere, but in single-mindedness her stepdaughter was a match for her. 'My beloved mother', she wrote to Uncle Simon, 'often invites me to other fields of labour, but I cannot abandon this till I see it my duty... Will none of my cousins become missionaries?', she asked him, gently passing the buck if not the baton. 'I long to see a Kilham rise up in that station'.[2] On Hannah's second missionary journey, to Sierra Leone in 1827-28, she had concentrated on visits to schools for children of liberated slaves. Slavery was still an issue. Parliament had outlawed the trade in 1807, but it would not be abolished in the Dominions until 1833, and even then abolition would take a few years to implement. Now she wanted to develop her ideas about teaching African children in their mother tongue by the Lancasterian method – already tried out briefly in the Gambia in 1824 – in a school of her own.[3] Sarah had something which she lacked: many years of precisely this kind of experience, with Russian girls, as well as more recent sustained practice in running a school. It would be amazing if she did not dream of their working together. But this was not to be. Sarah had ears only for her call back to Russia.

Hannah and Sarah spent the summer of 1830 together.[4] Hannah resolved to return to Sierra Leone, without the sponsorship of a missionary society or of the Society of Friends, whose Committee for African

Instruction she herself had generated ten years earlier; when in the previous summer a further visit was discussed, its members had been cordial but disposed to put the matter off for a year.[5] She did not raise it again but financed herself, with some help from individual supporters. Her much younger friend Elizabeth Hodgkin – daughter of Luke Howard, who was a leading Tottenham Quaker and former staunch ally of Hannah's estranged by the collapse of the Committee's Gambian project of 1823-24 and her role in it[6] – passed on news of her: 'Some kind friends in London have on this occasion had the charge of fitting her out, aided by the very efficient help of her daughter *[sic]*, S. Kilham, who has been on a visit to her native land for some months past'. Hannah, she had heard, had felt more 'comfortable' on this occasion than on either of the two former ones.[7]

Sarah was to have a similar impression. She had gone with Hannah to Gravesend to see the ship, the *Thomas Wallace*, which was expected to take her to Sierra Leone, and Hannah's fear of the water was only too obvious on the boat out to it. Sarah had dreaded the day of parting, perhaps forever in this life (as indeed it would prove to be), but felt 'mercifully sustained' and thankful for having been with her and watched 'her close walk with God'. On that final occasion at Gravesend 'we bade each other farewell in a peace and calmness which could only be bestowed by Omnipotence'.[8] Hannah set sail on 17 October; this time the voyage took over two months. She started a school for the daughters of liberated slaves in the village of Charlotte, and her biographer describes this period as 'among the happiest of Hannah Kilham's life'.[9] Despite frustrations, hardships and health problems, she showed greater staying power than on previous visits to the field. She ran her school with the help of a gifted matron, pioneered mother-tongue teaching and distributed her materials in other local communities. Early in 1832 she decided to make a trip to Liberia, the adjacent American colony settled with former slaves, to spread her educational ideas and practices. On the way back she fell sick. She died on 31 March 1832, aged 58, and was buried at sea.[10]

Meanwhile Sarah Kilham, having helped her stepmother to prepare for her final journey to Africa and said a last good-bye, had more family business on her hands. She heard that a new biography of her father was contemplated. A 'Life' had been published soon after Alexander Kilham's death: *The Life of Mr Alexander Kilham, Methodist Preacher...*, by himself and edited by John Grundell and Robert Hall with additional material. Two years later he had an entry in Charles Atmore's *The Methodist Memorial*. Now the prospective biographer was John Blackwell. Sarah gave him a collection of pamphlets which her father had either written or commented on. Blackwell evidently monitored the whereabouts of Alexander's personal papers and wrote to Sarah as soon as he decently could after Hannah's death.

Hannah had made a will before her 1827 voyage to Sierra Leone. She had bequeathed some money to her niece Hannah Corbett, then 17, who had perhaps been named after her, and commended her to Sarah's care. This must have been rather difficult to exercise from St Petersburg, but perhaps it reflected Hannah's hope of Sarah's return. Otherwise she had left her whole estate to Sarah.[11] This therefore included her father's manuscripts and letters. They were despatched to St Petersburg, then she sent them back across the sea to Blackwell.[12] He put them to excellent use in his anonymous *Life of the Rev. Alexander Kilham*, a study which despite the sententious wordiness of its period has never been surpassed for the careful and comprehensive treatment of its subject.

Representing Richard

We have already identified Sarah as the mysterious 'zealous female' to whom the British and Foreign Bible Society had made a grant of Scriptures in 1829. She took advantage of her year in England to correspond more freely with the Society and to do business on behalf of Richard Knill. Referring to the grant, she wrote:

> ...a few remain in the hands of two Englishmen and a Russian priest for distribution, the rest have when practicable been sold either at the full price or lower and a number have been given to poor English, German & French residents including some as rewards to the children in the foreign School & colonist children residing in the neighbouring villages.

'Colonist' refers to German settlements. She forwarded the proceeds: £10 15s 11d. She also commented that the Minister of Finance had exempted the books from the usual customs duty as they were for charitable use.[13] This goes to show that, despite the personal need for secrecy and the hostility of the likes of Metropolitan Serafim, there were still people in high places who not only acknowledged the legitimacy of the new Protestant Bible Society but also encouraged activities such as it undertook. Inconsistency was rife and because you could not be sure you had to be careful.

Six months later Sarah wrote to the BFBS again:

> Hoping to return to St Petersburg in spring & being likely soon to leave London I should esteem it a particular favour if there could be entrusted to me a few small French Bibles, together with some English Testaments in a larger type for the aged poor – some small English Bibles, & a few pearl Testaments with the psalms subjoined.

'Pearl' must have meant the tiny 5-point type-size. She enclosed a translation of a letter in Latin from Nils Gustaf Malmberg to Richard Knill (asking to be remembered to Miss 'Sara Chilom'), about his receipt of Finnish New Testaments. Malmberg was a young man whom she had met in St Petersburg in 1829. Recently ordained, he was now stationed at Kalajoki in Finland. In his reply Mr Jackson of the BFBS offered to supply Malmberg with Finnish Testaments from Stockholm if it was inappropriate for Knill to do so from St Petersburg – again we sense a fear of treading on eggshells – and to provide her or Knill with 25 of each of the Bibles requested plus 50 pearl Testaments with psalters.[14]

Sarah Kilham continued to make herself useful to Richard Knill, trying to arrange for him to receive the *Evangelical Magazine*, forwarding various reports and in particular acting as his go-between in financial matters. Getting money to him was complicated, but what seems to have happened was that his sponsors, the London Missionary Society, paid sums to Sarah which she transferred to him through drafts on their mutual friend, Archibald Mirrielees,[15] the man who had previously brought prospective pupils to her when their mother was gaoled.

Friends and Relations

Archibald was not only a friend of Sarah's, he had become a relation by proxy. Born in 1797, he was an Aberdonian, short in height, short in temper and very energetic. In his mid-teens he had moved to London, working as a clerk for Fisher & Co., and in 1822 became their representative in St Petersburg. He joined Richard Knill's congregation and made friends with William Gellibrand and William Spurr, Hannah Kilham's nephew, also in business there.[16] William Spurr was the son of Peter junior, who had married Hannah Newbould of the well-known file-making family in Sheffield in 1798. It is quite possible that William served as a link between Sarah Kilham and members of the British Congregation some years before she transferred her allegiance. In 1824, however, he fell ill, and his father and sister, another Sarah, travelled from Sheffield to be with him. Sadly, he died on 1 August, aged 26, before they could reach him.[17] While they were in St Petersburg, however, Archibald fell in love with Sarah Newbould Spurr. (Or perhaps this just confirmed a mutual attraction sparked off during an 1823 visit by Sarah, if she had been the Miss Spurr, 'the good young creature', who had called on the Knills before returning home.)[18] Two years later Archibald paid a visit to her family in Sheffield to secure parental consent, and in February 1828 he was there again to marry her at the Parish Church and take her back with him to the Russian capital. Thus it came about that our Sarah lost one resident step-cousin only to gain another, plus three little step-cousins once removed by 1835.[19]

Sarah's other activities during her year in England are cloaked in obscurity. It is highly likely that she visited her friends and adoptive family on the southern outskirts of Sheffield, yet there is no record of this. Hannah Kilham's brother Peter Spurr, Master Cutler in 1824 as their father had been in 1781, appears to have taken over the older Peter's business as maker of pen and pocket knives. Moving from Church Street to 56 Arundel Street in 1794, the firm had expanded into household and surgical instruments such as corkscrews, toothpicks, lancets and phlemes (lancets for treating horses).[20]

The 1825 directory is the first to describe Peter junior as a merchant as well as a manufacturer, with his residence at Heeley Bank in the Park.[21] This development of his business would easily explain why his sons were in St Petersburg. By 1833 he seems to have entirely given up manufacturing in favour of marketing and to have acquired or assumed higher status along the way, for he is described as 'gentleman' with his office at 1 Eyre Lane.[22] At Heeley Bank he became a gentleman farmer, calling himself 'formerly Merchant, now Farmer' in his will of 1836.[23] Peter gave his surname to the eastern third of Myrtle Road, the section from Heeley Green to East Bank Road, still known as Spurr Lane in the early 1930s. The substantial farmhouse was half way along this street, opposite the drive to Ash Farm adjoining the former Sheffield United practice ground.[24] Peter Spurr died in the summer of 1838.

Soon after her arrival Sarah was staying at the house of John Burll, 10 Haberdashers Place, Hoxton, then on the outskirts of London.[25] There is a remnant of this street close to Pitfield Street, N1, near the eastern end of Haberdasher Street. Mora Dickson was almost certain that Hannah was living in Elder Street, Spitalfields the previous autumn.[26] Just north-west of Spitalfields Market, then smaller, this was well under a mile from Haberdashers Place. If Hannah was still there, contact would be easy.

In February 1831 Sarah made a journey to the north-west to see friends and Hannah's relations. A letter about this is rare and short enough to justify quoting in full. It was addressed to Thomas Thompson, Druggist, Church Street, Liverpool. His business was at no. 80 in what remains Liverpool's foremost shopping street. The Thompsons, let us recall, were Quakers, long-standing friends and correspondents of Hannah's; their daughter Mary had been a pupil at the Sheffield boarding school.

My dear Friend,

   Having to pass through Liverpool in my way to Southport it would give me much pleasure to spend a night or two with you if perfectly convenient. I have prepared to go to Liverpool by the ten o'clock steam coaches on Saturday morning. Should I be asking too much by requesting a line to know if this be received – I am at Matthew Corbett's, Pendleton near Manchester.

I have heard with interest of dear Mary's being *[word(s) missing, document frayed]* as a Mistress of a family. May she be happy & be the instrument of happiness to others.

We have had no intelligence of the arrival of my beloved Mother in Africa, yet as the winds have been fair we hope she is now labouring among a people she so dearly loves.

> With dear love to you all / I am
> thy affectionate friend
> Sarah Kilham.[27]

There are several points of interest in this letter. Sarah still writes as if she were a Quaker, and we have the impression that nobody minds enough that she is no longer formally in membership to raise it as an issue. Ties of friendship override denominational ones. The Corbetts were family; we remember that Hannah's 'niece' Ann Corbett of Manchester had been on her school staff and had briefly taken charge. She was the stepdaughter of Hannah's younger sister, yet another Sarah, baptised on 14 January 1776, and like Hannah a Quaker 'by convincement'. Sarah Spurr had become Matthew Corbett's third wife in 1805. She bore him nine children of whom five survived childhood.[28]

Matthew sounds an interesting character. His father Moses was a shoe-maker of Middleham in North Yorkshire, but Matthew appears to have worked in the Isle of Man, for in 1791 his Quaker membership was transferred to Manchester from Peel. He was described as a cotton manufac-turer in 1802 and as a builder when he married Sarah Spurr.[29] The Friends came to think that he had cast his business net too widely when in 1819 he became insolvent, and as usual a committee investigated the case. Against debts of £12,182, he owned stock worth £2748 and real prop-erty valued at £4590, leaving a deficit of £4844, close to £325,000 in what it could buy in 2008.[30] The focus of the problem was his cotton enterprise, its main cause was lack of capital, and its unacceptable con-sequence was that his creditors suffered. So Hardshaw East (Manchester) Monthly Meeting disowned him, which he did not take meekly, asking for the evidence against him.[31]

Matthew, Sarah and their youngest daughter Martha then departed for Alexandria, District of Columbia, an important and historic com-mercial centre now in Virginia, USA. We do not know all the circum-stances of this, but according to James Montgomery Hannah's sister 'went once to the United States' as a religious teacher. In 1824 they returned and Sarah and Martha rejoined the Meeting, but Matthew never did.[32] In 1831 Pendleton Friends attended the brand-new meeting house in

Mount Street, which now stands behind Manchester Central Library, built about a hundred years later.

Aged about 65 at the time of Sarah Kilham's visit, Matthew is described in a contemporary directory as a land and building agent, and elsewhere as a builder. The Corbetts lived at 1, Pimlott Street,[33] off Broad Street and facing Frederick Road. (Quite close to the site of the University of Salford, Pimlott Street was razed in the late 1960s.) Ten of Matthew's fifteen children reached adulthood. Two who recur in our story are Hannah, her namesake's favourite niece, and Elizabeth, from the second marriage. They will provide important clues to help us solve a mystery surrounding our Sarah's death. As for Hannah Kilham, she had landed in Freetown nearly two months earlier, but no word had yet been heard because there had been no returning ships. This gives us an abrupt reminder of the pace of international communications in that era.

The reference to steam coaches is fascinating. The famous Liverpool and Manchester Railway had been open just five months and it would be nice to think of Sarah as a pioneering rail passenger, but public steam carriages began to appear on the roads at this time too. The local press, however, makes no mention whatsoever of steam road carriages in Manchester, so we can only suppose that in February 1831 they were confined to the London area and Gloucestershire.[34] Sarah must have gone by train. We may be mildly surprised that she used the expression 'steam coaches', but this was quite normal in the days of railway infancy. The very earliest advertisements and reports spoke not of trains but of railway carriages, first-class coaches and second-class coaches, and only a few months later of 'trains of carriages' or simply trains.[35]

Initially passenger trains between Manchester and Liverpool were either first-class or second, not combined. Sarah's 10 o'clock 'coach' from Liverpool Road Station, off Deansgate, is likely to have been a first-class one. Not only was the term 'carriage' used interchangeably with 'coach', but those original first-class carriages actually looked like a series of stage coaches, three coach bodies forming three compartments joined into a single carriage on an iron underframe with four wheels. They were painted black above and yellow below. As well as the company's name they carried one of their own such as 'Queen Adelaide', again just like stage coaches, probably to help passengers find their booked seats. These cost 7s one way in a compartment for four, 5s in one for six. The literal equivalent of 7s is 35p, but 7s in 1831 would have bought about £25 worth of goods and services in 2008.[36] Sarah was clearly not short of money. First-class travel was decidedly expensive and second-class fares were not exactly cheap. The reason was that both were meant for better-off people. The masses very seldom went by train until third class was introduced forty years later, soon ousting second.

Sarah climbed in by means of folding steps, assisted by an attendant (the guard or brakesman) who put her luggage on the roof – with no more than an iron railing to protect it – and took his own seat there on the front end of the carriage, as if he were the driver. She found more reminders of stage coaches inside the compartment with its light brown upholstery and its curtained windows. On second-class trains the carriages were painted blue, with a single fare of 3s 6d in what amounted to an open truck with seats, but by March 1831 there were already 'glass coaches' too where you paid as much as in a first-class six-person compartment. Trains took from an hour and forty minutes to two hours to reach Liverpool's Crown Street Station,[37] long gone. Its site, now in the main university area, was then on the fringe of the city.

Why Sarah was on her way to Southport she does not tell us. By this date Quakers were meeting there in a private house,[38] but she mentions no names of mutual friends to the Thompsons. Established at the end of the eighteenth century, the tiny Lancashire resort had recently been dubbed the Montpellier of England, to the scorn of its local historian.[39] A plan of 1824, calling it the Hamlet of South Port, shows the beginnings of Lord Street – now the main thoroughfare and an attractive boulevard – but very little else. It had three hotels, some boarding houses and a hot bath.[40] Sarah most likely visited Southport for the health-giving properties ascribed to it. A journey from London to the north-west of England could hold no terrors for a woman who had travelled from London to the north-west of Russia.

Sarah also went to Epworth for a few days to see her father's family, and back in St Petersburg in October she would write a belated thank-you letter to Uncle Simon: 'I ever remember your kind and cordial reception of me'.[41] He had been described in March 1830 as 'a leader and steward in our society at Epworth',[42] so it is likely that she visited the New Connexion's Providence Chapel of 1803-4 in Church Street to admire the extensions of 1820.[43] The chapel could now accommodate some 300 people, although if the situation was as it would be two decades later the building would rarely be more than half full.[44] It was a similar picture elsewhere. Sarah's other uncles, the elusive farmer Richard and the dour clockmaker and preacher Thomas, had both died in 1826.

In her letter Sarah was to pass on news of Hannah at her school in Charlotte, Sierra Leone. She also sent her Epworth cousins good wishes which quickly became an exhortatory mini-sermon:

> I hope my dear cousins are well in body, and more and more earnestly pursuing heavenly treasure, more and more feeling that whether we eat or drink or whatever we do, we ought to do all to the glory of GOD, and more and more considering time, health,

money and opportunities of doing good as talents committed to them for which they *must* give an account in the last day.[45] And so on. One wonders whether admonitions of this kind had become second nature to Sarah, irrespective of their targets, or whether the cousins or some of them had done something to deserve them. The law of averages might suggest the latter: Thomas had been childless, but Simon and Richard had between them produced about fifteen cousins then living – Simon three with his first wife Mary and seven with his second wife Ann – their ages ranging from late teens to early forties. Given Sarah and her background, they probably accepted her exhortations as par for the course.

Notes and References

1   Biller, ed., p 366.
2   SK, *NMM*, 33 (1830), p 278.
3   For the Gambia: Dickson, pp 159-61; for how this was to be realized: ibid., pp 221-5, 233, 238.
4   Biller, ed., p 365.
5   Dickson, pp 111-13, 213-14, 217.
6   Ibid., pp 113-14, 189, 216.
7   [J. Hodgkin Jr, comp.,] *Extracts from the Familiar Letters of the Late Elizabeth Hodgkin* (London, 1842), pp 68-9.
8   Biller, ed., pp 365-6.
9   Dickson, p 219.
10 Ibid., pp 222, 226-9, 234-5, 239-40.
11 TNA: Prob 11/1810 f 262; niece's age from V.A. Oldham's indexes to births, marriages and deaths, Hardshaw Meeting (printout at Liverpool RO).
12 Blackwell, pp iv-v.
13 BSA/D1/2/31, SK to Josiah Forster, 3 July 1830.
14 CWM, Russia, RK's Journal, p 298; BSA/D1/2/33, Cornelius Rahmn to SK, 5 Jan 1831 and SK to John Jackson, 8 Jan 1831; BSA/D1/4/1/15, Jackson to SK, 11 Jan 1831.
15 CWM, Russia, In. Corr., 2/3/C, RK to W.A. Hankey, 14 Oct and 21 Dec 1830; 2/4/A, same to same, 23 Feb 1831; RK's Journal, p 298.
16 Pitcher, pp 2-5, 14.
17 Ibid, p 14; CWM, Russia, RK's Journal, pp 83, 87-9; FHL: Gibson IV/109, HK to Mrs Thomas Thompson, 6 Sep 1825.
18 CWM, Russia, RK's Journal, p 59.
19 Pitcher, pp 14, 16.
20 Gales and Martin's *Directory of Sheffield 1787*, p 15; Robinson's *Directory of Sheffield 1797*, p 116; Leader, 1 (1905), p 189. Full details of directories are given in the List of Sources.
21 Gell's *Directory of Sheffield 1825*, p 79.
22 White's *Directory of Sheffield 1833*, p 264.
23 SA: LD 2006 (94).

24 H. Tatton, 'Old Sheffield: Sketches and Notes, 1920-1936', 3, p 518 (pho-
    tocopy of manuscript); Heeley History Workshop, *Heeley and Thereabouts*
    (Sheffield, 2004), pp 14, 61.
25 CWM, Russia, RK's Journal, p 293.
26 Dickson, p 216.
27 FHL: Gibson V/207, SK to [Mrs?] Thomas Thompson, 16 Feb 1831; Gore's
    Directory of Liverpool (Liverpool, 1834), p 346.
28 Oldham's indexes.
29 MCL: MF PR 938.
30 Derived from rates for 2007 at www.measuringworth.com, accessed in 2008.
31 MCL: M85/2/1/1 pp 123-4, 129-31, 134-5.
32 MCL: M85/2/7/1, f 47; M85/2/8, p 77; Holland and Everett, 5, p 157.
33 Pigot's *Directory of Manchester 1832*, pp 74, 316; MCL: Index to Deeds.
    Hannah refers to Matthew as her brother-in-law in her will (TNA: Prob
    11/1810 f 262). His wife Sarah appears in the 1841 census.
34 R.H. Clark, 'The Steam Engine in Industry and Road Transport', in
    Engineering Heritage, 1 (London, 1963), pp 66-7; J. Hibbs, *The History of
    British Bus Services*, 2nd rev. edn (Newton Abbot, 1989), p 20.
35 *Manchester Courier* (hereafter *MC*), especially 25 Sept 1830, 5 and 26 Feb
    1831.
36 Derived from rates for 2007 at www.measuringworth.com, accessed in 2008.
37 R.H.G. Thomas, *The Liverpool & Manchester Railway* (London, 1980), pp
    180-2; fares and journey times from *MC*, 25 Sept 1830 and 26 Feb 1831.
38 F.A. Bailey, *A History of Southport* (Southport, 1955, repr. 1992), p 113.
39 Ibid., p 53.
40 Ibid., pp 24-5, 59, 90.
41 SK, *NMM*, 35 (1832), p 81.
42 W. Baggaley, note to letter from SK, *NMM*, 33 (1830), p 277.
43 Rose, 'The First Methodist', p 15.
44 R.A. Ambler, ed., *Lincolnshire Returns of the Census of Religious Worship 1851*,
    Lincoln Record Society, 72 (no place, 1979), p 273.
45 SK, *NMM*, 35 (1832), p 82; her emphasis.

5. BECOMING MRS BILLER

SARAH'S SECOND RUSSIAN DECADE

Adding an Infant School

ON 4 MAY 1831 Richard Knill recorded in his journal that Miss Kilham had arrived at Kronstadt.[1] Feelings of pleasurable anticipation of meeting her charges and friends again were, we suspect, mingled with a certain apprehension. Russia and more particularly St Petersburg were where she saw the continuing course of her career. 'The school is small, but I trust it will prove a seed of future usefulness; and if by much labour, time and anxiety I should at last see education become generally established on sound principles, I should think a life even well spent in the effort', she had written in 1827.[2] But her school was in the personal gift of the Emperor, the Autocrat; she was a foreigner; and she remembered, not long before, the fall of the Russian Bible Society and its ministerial president Prince Golitsyn.

The public allegedly branded Golitsyn 'the protector of Quakers and Methodists', who 'were working to obtain as much influence as possible on public education'.[3] What prompted D.P. Runich, Curator of the St Petersburg Educational District from 1821 until his enforced retirement in 1826, scourge of its university and the author of these words, to install Methodists in the pillory too is interesting to speculate upon. It would be tempting to think that Runich had Knill and the schoolmaster Gray in mind and found that 'metodisty' tripped more readily off the tongue or the pen than a Russian version of Congregationalists. Knill himself wrote that many strenuously opposed his school for poor foreign children, 'especially as it is in the hands of those whom they are pleased to style "Methodists"'.[4]

In fact, Runich just took the term as shorthand for Protestant nonconformity. His colleague, M.L. Magnitsky, went further, using it to mean mystics and evangelicals, not only Britons or other foreigners but sometimes Russians who shared their ideas. In a report of 1831 to the Emperor, equalling a dozen printed pages, the words 'Methodism' and 'Methodists' occur two dozen times. Methodists now would be startled to find themselves described as 'the Jesuits of the Anglican confession',[5] but Magnitsky was in fact parroting a charge formerly levelled by Wesley's critics at his followers. In England too, following the French Revolution, Methodists were accused of Jacobinism, bent on overturning the established order, church and state alike. (This was an important reason why the vast majority of their leaders wanted to disown Alexander Kilham.) Even the evangelical Hannah More, no Methodist, found herself attacked and branded with that name for setting up Sunday schools.[6] Magnitsky linked these stories of subversion with what had been happening in the Russian capital. The 'celebrated preacher Knill', he asserted, had come to St Petersburg with the aim of enticing English people away from the Church of England. He had preached to an 'extraordinary throng' of English, Germans and Russians; among them was Princess Meshcherskaya, 'a founder of the Bible Society in Moscow and publisher of translations of Methodist booklets'.[7]

These tracts 'expounded the Methodist dogma that, in order to convert and save the most hardened sinner, neither the Church nor her mysteries *[sacraments]* are necessary, only the wonderful action of God'.[8] (Magnitsky is over the top as usual, but here for once he draws somewhat closer to real-life Methodism, which has always defined salvation primarily in terms of personal response to the Gospel.) Magnitsky's implicit concern was that this undermined Orthodoxy, as did the 'Methodist'-dominated Bible Society through its principle of issuing the Scriptures without (Orthodox) commentary. Popov, Paterson and Pinkerton were denounced along with many others, as were Lancasterian schools, but Sarah Kilham, James Heard and the Wheelers came off lightly. This was arguably because they had friends in very high places, they were valued and it was hard to criticize what they were actually doing:

> Here I shall mention neither the Quakers who have headed their own schools in St Petersburg, nor their settlement along the Tsarskoe Selo road, under the patronage and direction of Privy Counsellor Dzhunkovsky, a Methodist of long standing.[9]

The real patron of Sarah's school was to be the Emperor's sister-in-law.

In any event, as we saw earlier, Sarah need not have worried. She reported to Uncle Simon:

> I am again placed in the school I have lived in for ten years, and again rejoice to be among my dear children. I was as kindly as possibly received by the wife of the Emperor's brother; and desired by her to do all I could for the poor, as well as take care of the present school, and form an Infant school under the same roof... I feel here much more at home than I did while in England, and am glad once more to be allowed to labour among these children.[10]

Sarah's new patron, 'the wife of the Emperor's brother', was the young Grand Duchess Elena Pavlovna (1806-73), married to Nicholas I's younger brother Michael. Of German origin, she had caused a sensation, on her arrival at court as his 16-year-old bride-to-be, by her self-confidence and sharpness of intellect.[11] She was liberal in her political views, favouring for example the emancipation of the serfs,[12] which lay 30 years ahead. Even while Nicholas was still alive – he held that the battlefield was no place for women – she was to achieve the remarkable feat of overcoming his iron will and setting up a corps of nursing volunteers to serve in the Crimean War under the direction of Russia's leading doctor N. Pirogov.[13] With a heart for philanthropic institutions for women and children, she and Sarah would get on well.

Grand Duchess Elena Pavlovna in 1824.

In mid-June 1831 preparations for the new infants' school were dramatically interrupted:

> ...the Cholera broke out and stopped all our movements. This has been a very awful visitation, and thousands have fallen victims to its ravages. Through infinite mercy we have been preserved! Oh! may the solemn feelings experienced when death appeared at the elbow of each of us – when we felt how uncertain it was whether from meal to meal the family would still all assemble together – when we truly could form no plan for the morrow – oh! may these feelings of the vanity of the world, and the reality of eternity, ever be as engraven on the palms of our hands... not one of my intimate friends has fallen, although several most courageously and most benevolently were led to devote themselves to the nursing and caring for the sick.[14]

Not all of Sarah's acquaintances were spared, and not all of her closest friends were unaffected. Mrs Chapman, mistress at Knill's school, died on 27 July, and her little orphan daughter was taken by Mrs Elizabeth Gellibrand to live with her. Richard, with other members of the school committee, accompanied the body to the cholera burial ground and conducted the funeral service, surrounded by coffins. On 30 July his little son Joseph fell ill. He lived four more days but meanwhile his brother Johnny had died. When Richard's wife Sarah also became sick, Sarah Mirrielees took charge of Samuel, the last of the Knill children, until she recovered.[15]

The epidemic eventually subsided, and early in October Sarah Kilham was able to open her new infant school. Four years previously she had had 20 boarders and about the same number of day pupils.[16] Now they had more than doubled. As she wrote to Epworth:

> We have a large school, forty-two children living in the house; thirty day scholars in the girls' school; and twelve in the infant school. This latter school has only been opened three weeks; and as it is the first of its kind, it has to make its own way. I feel little doubt but if nothing else induces mothers to send their little ones, the comfort of being rid of them seven or eight hours in a day will have some influence. So far these little ones are getting forward very nicely.[17]

Also they were kept away from the dangers of the streets.

As Sarah herself has made clear, 'infant school' here means a department, not a separate building. It is interesting that she describes it as an innovation. If her claim is correct, she must certainly be credited with being the first person to *found* such a school in St Petersburg, but it is unclear from the above record of her interview with the Emperor's sister-in-law whose *idea* it was. There were already schools like this in England, but Elena Pavlovna with her German background may well have known about the school for small children that was in existence in Berlin by 1830; it was followed by 29 other 'Kleinkinderschulen' by 1847, catering for ages 2 to 6.[18] In the winter of 1833/34 Elena Pavlovna herself opened, in her palace, an infant school for the children of the palace servants.[19]

Whether the Berlin influence preceded or succeeded the establishment of Sarah's infant school, it had certainly made its mark by 1839, when she wrote to William Allen:

> Schools are increasing, particularly the Berlin Infant Schools, or rather asylums for little children, while their parents go to work. It is to be hoped these will do much good, for it is of great consequence that little children should be inured to order, neatness and exertion.[20]

She now took the welfare function of the infant schools for granted, and in any case it was implicit in the term 'asylums', meaning refuges. Her own school – not just the infants' department – had been increasing too. 'Our school is going on much as formerly, we have between thirty and forty boarders, and more than one hundred children in daily attendance'.[21] This, the latest record of her pupil numbers that we have found, represents a growth rate of about 60 per cent since 1831. The rise in admissions was matched by a widening of the school's unofficial catchment area. Thus, writing in 1841 to John Venning, she commented that while at one time they were glad if girls came from the neighbouring streets, they now had them coming daily from places like Vasil'evsky Island across the Neva, and the girls took the distance for granted. She ascribed this to an increasing desire in St Petersburg to have girls educated,[22] but modestly refrained from thoughts about the reputation of her school.

Sarah Gets Married

Resolute readers of our references will have noticed that SK has become SB. There was not the faintest hint in Sarah's letter of 24 October 1831 to Uncle Simon that in less than three months' time she would be walking down the aisle to be married. It is another sign of her great reticence on personal matters, unless of course William Biller had still to pop the question. This is unlikely because Sarah was not one for rushing into major decisions. To give an example: even though Daniel Wheeler had judged her first arrival in St Petersburg in September 1820 to be over-hasty, we know that she had been thinking over her dramatic career change since some date in 1819 when Alexander's invitation of March had reached the Kilhams by the Quaker grapevine. They had certainly been writing to each other in the spring when William was in Moscow. He was the anonymous 'friend' she quoted in a letter to the Bible Society.[23] However the proposal came about, here is the outcome as recorded in the Anglican register for 1832:

> William Biller, Bachelor, of the Lutheran Congregation, and Sarah Kilham, Spinster, of this Congregation, were married by Banns, according to the Rites of the Church of England, on the 14th day of January, by me, Edward Law, Minister.

This marriage was solemnised between Us	In the presence of Us
William Biller	Archibald Merrilies
Sarah Kilham	W.C. Gellibrand
	S.N. Merrilies
	Eliz[h] Gellibrand[24]

This entry begs for comment. There is nothing surprising about Sarah being married in the St Petersburg Anglican church. Once William and Sarah had agreed that they should have an English service, they had no further choice, because Richard Knill did not conduct marriages. Before the Marriage Act of 1836, marriage ceremonies were legally valid in England only if they were Anglican, Jewish or Quaker; English people living abroad usually wanted to secure this legality if they could. Sarah was no longer a professing Quaker so the problem of 'marrying out', not allowed until about 1860, did not arise.[25] The surprise lies in the description of Sarah as 'of this Congregation', as she was still a member of Knill's. Perhaps Edward Law was relaxed about such things, using 'of this Congregation' in the same way and with the same mind-set as he would have used 'of this Parish' if based in England. The list of witnesses suggests an intimate gathering of the nonconformist family. It was just as well that there was no foreknowledge to mar the rejoicing: Elizabeth Gellibrand, her husband's first wife, would die in the terrible winter of 1832/33, and Sarah Newbould Mirrielees, Archibald's first wife and Hannah Kilham's niece, was to follow her late in 1835.[26] But the main question is: who was the mysterious Mr Biller? Richenda Scott said that nothing was known of him except that he was certainly not a Friend. She gave his name as Samuel.[27] Presumably both statements, the first correct and the second not, stemmed from the absence of any eligible Mr Biller from the Quaker records; she derived 'Samuel' from Jane Benson. Scott's successor, who included Russia in his Quaker history, surmised that he was an affluent member of the German community.[28] He gave no source for this – perhaps it was just the sound of the name – but there is some circumstantial evidence to support him.

Firstly, William Biller's allegiance to the Lutherans as recorded in Mr Law's register suggests that he was German, or possibly Dutch or Scandinavian. Secondly, one of his few surviving letters contains distinctly German touches. The assumption is that his wife normally cast her eye over them but on this occasion she did not. For example: 'Bishop T...', who died 1783 [no preposition] aged 59 years, is a very favourite [?ein sehr beliebter] author'. William is at his oddest when translating from Russian to English: 'he who curiously dives in the nature of God... Avoid O man to unravel what has been withholden from thee'.[29] Here too is a German construction; we would say 'avoid unravelling', in the unlikely event that we used such a word! Thirdly, although he does not appear in person in the infrequently published St Petersburg directories, the 1824 one includes a Yugan (probably baptised Jürgen) Ernst Biller, merchant, who may well have been a close relation.[30] He sounds like a foreigner, and foreign merchants tended to be quite well off. Was William, or had he been, a merchant in the same concern? Between 1831 and 1835 he speaks of making trips to Moscow,[31] which may have been primarily on business, although he refers to these in other contexts. He also mentions a very recent visit to 'one of our near relations', almost certainly in St Petersburg, who showed them a new edition of the Lutheran Bible.[32] We may suppose that he let himself be known as William to fit in more easily with his English-speaking friends. He proved even more elusive when enquiries were made about him at the Munich databank on German residents in Russia.[33]

William Biller first figured in our story as a contributor to Richard Knill's good causes. These appearances were in 1828-29, and we may infer from the size of the donations that he could afford to be liberal. In January 1831 he came to assist Richard 'in making up the Books', and later in the year his and Sarah's names occurred for the first time together as subscribers to a special fund for shipwrecked English sailors who had turned up in the capital.[34] So William had already been acquainted with Richard's congregation for a few years, though probably remaining an adherent rather than becoming a member, for he is not included with Sarah in a list of members of 1833.[35] She was just 43 when they married. His age is not known.

The Billers and the Bible Society

There is only one aspect of the married life of Sarah and William that is well documented: their shared enthusiasm for the work of the British and Foreign Bible Society. That by focussing on this we may exaggerate its importance to them is a danger we cannot avoid. It began at home: we have a nice little vignette of William bringing the Good News to the school servants:

> The two men we have for chopping wood, fetching water &c have each their large Bible which they carefully preserve & study when their labour is ended. My Husband reads to them & questions them on Sabbath days from the sacred writings & it is quite cheering to see the heartiness & pleasure evinced in their thanks at the close of each reading.[36]

They also ran an informal religious library for some of their callers,[37] and were in the habit of visiting German Christians. Sarah wrote that she did not understand the language and could not determine their denomination but she much enjoyed their weekend evening meetings. They sound like what we would now call a house church, but a large one attracting 100-200 people.[38]

William's particular targets in his Bible Society activities were soldiers and prisoners. John Jackson, the Secretary, often urged his correspondents to supply material illustrating the success of their work (and mildly livening up the pages of the *Annual Reports*). The following will serve as an example of the anecdotes favoured by William and Sarah alike:

> When in Moscow in May 1831 I met with a young soldier in the government shop where the Scriptures & religious publications are sold & asked him whether he had either a Testament or Psalter. He answered negatively so I told him I would give them to him if he chose to walk home with me. He informed me on the way that he frequented four churches as often as his time would admit in order to join in the chanting *without being paid.* He could not write; he had taught himself to read, his mother having merely acquainted him with the alphabet. When we reached my lodgings I gave him a Testament, a Psalter and some tracts; he obliged me to write my

name in the Testament & when I had done that he requested me to write the name of my parents & relations also, in order to remember us all at a throne of grace. Agitated by a sense of gratitude he on the point of parting laid hold of my hand to kiss it & closed with the words: 'God has sent you to me as an angel to give me these books'. – How often circumstances in themselves insignificant are overruled for the good of either ourselves or others! Had I come to the shop a quarter of an hour earlier or later I should very likely never have seen the soldier, for in the afternoon he was to leave Moscow.[39]

Divine Providence figures prominently in the reflections of both the Billers. They had apparently forgotten that Sarah had told the same story to Jackson fifteen months earlier in very similar words from a letter received from her husband-to-be in Moscow.[40] But if they felt that it was too good to leave out of the *Annual Report* and meant to jog Jackson's memory, they got nowhere with it.

Where the prisoners were concerned, Sarah assisted William in correspondence. He in turn supported Friedrich Joseph Haass (1780-1853), a German Catholic doctor who was very active in prison visiting as the hands-on director of the Moscow Society for the Care of Prisons.[41] He was better known in Moscow as Fyodor Petrovich Gaaz, 'the saintly doctor'.[42] The Muscovites drastically russianized his Christian names but they found the surname almost intractable. Originally an eye specialist, he was the Moscow City Physician for a few years and the chief medical officer of Moscow's prison hospitals for many more. His achievements in prison reform included, among much else, persuading the authorities to ban flogging and to ease the pain of shackles by halving their weight and lining them with leather. At least 20,000 people, it was said, attended his funeral.[43]

Prison visiting went hand in hand with the distribution of Bibles and tracts. The Bible Society and the Society for the Care of Prisons were organically linked through their committees.[44] A sequence of letters about these activities in 1833-34 reveals that neither the Billers nor the Bible Society suppliers showed any trace of anti-Catholic prejudice as they sought to spread the Word in Russia. The Bible Society resolutely refused to differentiate between denominations in that it not only published Protestant and Roman Catholic Testaments without commentary but also permitted the purchase of other publishers' Bibles meeting the same basic criterion.

Dr Haass had a special concern for French-, German- and Polish-speaking prisoners passing through Moscow into Siberian exile. (There had been an unsuccessful Polish rebellion against Russian rule in 1830-31.) Sarah originally asked for RC Testaments in French and German and John Jackson, acceding to her request, himself suggested applying for Polish versions. William referred his letter to Dr Haass. When Haass welcomed this, Sarah wrote for permission to buy from a stock of 400 Polish Catholic Testaments which had been found to be available in Moscow.[45] The Bible Society sanctioned the purchase of half of these, provided that they contained no extra matter and won the approval of Richard Knill. William subsequently bought the books in two instalments during his Moscow visits and handed them over to a grateful Dr Haass.[46] In the summer of 1835 he went round one of the prisons in the saintly doctor's company.[47]

For her part, Sarah regularly visited the women patients in a large St Petersburg hospital 'for those who have brought on themselves illness by disorderly conduct'. This is likely to be a euphemism for sexually transmitted diseases. All the wards had been supplied with Testaments in several different languages. She would see some of the women reading them, or listening to another person reading, and hope that the memory might 'draw some unhappy victim from the highway to perdition'. She would not, she wrote, depict the dark side of the picture.[48]

This brings us to a new sphere of interest for Sarah. In 1833, together with Anna Fyodorovna Mikhel'son (or Michelson), she set up a 'Magdalen refuge for fallen women'.[49] In several Christian countries the title Magdalen Institution or Asylum was used for such homes, springing from confusion between Mary Magdalene the follower of Jesus on the one hand and the penitent woman who anointed his feet in Luke 7:37-8 on the other. Sarah told her Bible Society contact that she and William had celebrated 1 August 1834 – the abolition of slavery in British colonies – by inviting 'the inmates of a small Magdalen recently opened' to spend the afternoon with them.[50] Hiding her light under the usual bushel, she did not reveal who had opened it.

John Venning had included such a facility among his philanthropic proposals, but back in 1828 it had remained on paper because of the Empress Mother's death. Sarah, however, regarded Venning as the inspiration for her refuge. In 1837, through Hannah Corbett, the step-cousin commended to her in Hannah Kilham's will, she sent him a copy of its current report. It was a shelter for girls who wanted to stop working the streets and probably also for patients discharged from the Kalinkin Hospital for venereal diseases, preparing them for employment in domestic service. 'Dear Mrs Michelson was the prompter and founder of the asylum', she wrote,[51] again underplaying her own role. Years later a Russian commentator would restore the balance, affirming that the Magdalen project had fully revealed Sarah's talent for organization and her ability to exert a healthy influence on the most stubborn personalities.[52]

Sarah's main function as an initially unofficial agent of the BFBS –
Richard Knill was the official one – was to oversee the reception of Biblical
materials from England and elsewhere and their distribution to various
parts of the Russian Empire. Places occurring in her lengthy letters include
Moscow, Astrakhan – a city of the deep south, nearly 1200 miles from St
Petersburg, in the delta where the Volga prepares to enter the Caspian
Sea – Finland and the St Petersburg area itself. Although Sarah refers several times to this activity, how exactly she went about it remains rather
obscure. She seems to have had a network of assistants, ranging from personal friends and acquaintances such as the Rev Matthew Camidge, minister at the British (Anglican) Chapel in Moscow, to an unnamed military
clerk who used to buy Testaments at subsidised prices and send them to
distant parts along with official despatches, and a peasant who claimed
that many of the books entrusted to him had covered up to 10,000 versts
from the capital. Given that 10,000 versts equal 6630 miles and that the
distance, for example, from St Petersburg to the southern central Siberian
city of Irkutsk, a famous place of exile and re-settlement at this time, is
some 2700 miles, Sarah's distributor seems to have been spinning her a
bit of a traveller's tale. It would still have been an overstatement if he had
gone further east and taken a circuitous route. She was also in the habit
of giving or selling Scriptural materials to individuals for their own use,
once obtaining a Bible in Church Slavonic for a young salesman in a local
shop.[53]

It was presumably a spin-off from her Bible Society work when Sarah
sent home a report on the Spiritual Christians (better known by their
Orthodox nickname Molokans, 'milk-eaters', referring to their consumption of dairy products on strict fast days).[54] She wrote:

> Lately two simple-minded Russian peasants called here from the
> interior. They dissent from the national religion, having cast off its
> ceremonies, and call themselves Spiritual Christians... The only
> account they can give [of their origins] is that being led to study the
> Scriptures they saw much in the usual [i.e. Orthodox] mode of wor-
> ship that was contrary to what appeared to them to be the truth –
> their hearts thirsted for a more spiritual way, and little by little they
> were led to collect in a body for worship.

Sarah went on to describe their worship, very Scripture-based with intervals of silent prayer, and their leadership by unsalaried itinerant elders.[55]
She seems to have been unaware that Allen and Grellet had visited a
Molokan settlement founded by the express permission of Alexander in
the south of Russia.[56]

Sarah also had an intermediary role in obtaining materials for the religious instruction of school pupils. In 1833 she wrote: 'I have by me just
now orders for the Infant School Scripture lessons for four schools on

estates at a distance belonging to the nobility'.[57] One wonders how these related to the lessons for older children compiled by Allen, Grellet and others and published with the late Emperor's enthusiastic backing in 1819. Certainly the basic principle in the selection of subject matter for the teaching of reading in the schools of mutual instruction was still as it had been then: 'no reading lessons are allowed except such as are drawn from the New Testament'. This was in fact more restricted than in the public parish schools, where excerpts from the Old Testament were also used.[58]

In 1834 we hear that the priest attached to Sarah's school was feeling frustrated by difficulties in understanding the Church Slavonic version. He looked forward with her to the day when the whole Bible would be available in Russian. She certainly regretted when selecting texts for RI that some themes which would have been perfectly clear in English had to be set aside because the Church Slavonic was so obscure. Meanwhile she was glad to have at least the New Testament and Psalms in the vernacular, as they contained all that was needful.[59]

Away from the school, Sarah had an occasional teaching engagement that was evidently very special for her. Using 'partially' in the old-fashioned sense of 'unduly', she wrote to Jackson in 1834:

> You may think I am partially attached to the Imperial family, indeed I have reason to be so, for since I resided in this country they have acted towards me as liberally as any human being could anticipate. My situation throws me into frequent communication with the second house in this land.

By this she meant the Grand Duke Michael's, and the palace she visited was the Mikhailovsky dvorets, completed in 1825 on Arts Square (ploshchad' Iskusstv) and now the Russian Museum, one of the country's two greatest galleries of Russian art. (It is not to be confused with the Mikhailovsky or Engineers' Castle (Inzhenersky zamok), built for Michael's father the Emperor Paul and better known for his violent death than for the few days of his life there.) The Grand Duchess, the liberally-minded Elena Pavlovna, as we may recall, was Sarah's patron and sometimes visited the school. One of her concerns was the religious knowledge both of Sarah's pupils and of her own children. She arranged for Sarah to give her two older ones, Maria, 9 and Elizaveta, 8, Russian scriptural texts from time to time, for them to translate into English and learn by heart. Sarah mentions going to see the eldest daughter.[60] As Elena Pavlovna was German and the court language was still French, these children must have been little polyglots.

Challenges for the Congregation

Sarah was witness to various developments affecting the British Congregation and their pastor at this time. A new venture for Richard was his preaching through the summer to British sailors 'on board the Bethel ship' at Kronstadt.[61] His members were still using the Moravian Meeting House in Great Stable Street (Bol'shaya Konyushennaya ulitsa, east of the Hermitage and just beyond the Moika); they nicknamed it 'the snuff box'. According to Harvey Pitcher the German brethren were so fond of snuff that the room had to be thoroughly aired – whatever the outside temperature – before Richard Knill's flock could venture inside.[62] This state of affairs was tiresome and eventually they decided to build their own chapel, taking up Richard's idea of a decade earlier which seems not to have elicited much of a response. In May 1833 Richard wrote to the Treasurer of the London Missionary Society, his employers, to tell him that the first hurdle had been overcome: 'the August Monarch has just now given us permission to build a Chapel expressly for the use of the Society of Congregationalists (a new word in the Russian language)'. He expected much friendly support from across the Atlantic, and the chapel would be called the Anglo-American Chapel.[63]

If Richard Knill was expecting like support from across the North Sea as he headed up the building project, however, he was about to get a big shock. The LMS suddenly told him they wanted him back in Britain to promote the Society's work there, for a limited period or permanently. His biographer thought that this stemmed in part from a wish to give him a change of scene after the tribulations of the cholera epidemic.[64] His members, alarmed, held a special meeting and sent a reasoned petition to London. While agreeing to his release for a year, they clearly felt that they might be at the thin end of a wedge (and they would be proved right): 'as a church we unanimously declare that we do not feel it our duty to lose the future labours of our present beloved & zealous shepherd, whose experience & standing in this country so peculiarly fit him for this station'. They cited a special reason for their stance: the recent building consent for a chapel, which meant that their status as a community of Congregationalists had been officially recognized, had been granted 'in the name of Mr Knill' (their emphasis) and the members. They feared that his leaving altogether might injure their cause.[65]

Richard himself, writing the following day, obviously felt that he ought to return to England immediately but there were practical grounds to consider. As superintendent of the charity school he should obtain from the Ministry of Education permission to leave and for his successor at the chapel to superintend the school in his absence. Another nine days and the Knills' departure was sealed.[66] Richard hoped at least that his presence in England would facilitate fund-raising there for the new chapel.[67]

Sarah Biller was among the 32 church members signing the petition, but William, as already mentioned, was not. This is probably because he was not technically in membership, although the absence of his name is no proof: Sarah Mirrielees did not sign it either. The signatories included her husband Archibald and his recently widowed friend W.C. Gellibrand. Most of the other names are unknown to us, though a few call for comment and one seems surprisingly familiar: who was the H. Spurr who signed – the same Henry from Sheffield, now grown up and back in business?

Whoever it was, that Henry Spurr definitely re-emerges. After his brother's death the family concern in St Petersburg was closed and he came back to England. A year later Hannah Kilham took it upon herself to write to her friend Frances Thompson in Liverpool, asking her to enquire about a job for him in some counting house there, 'in the mercantile or the shipping department'. 'I feel myself *indescribably* involved in a concern for his happiness', she wrote.[68] In 1851 we find Henry back in Sheffield, now a 'coal owner', residing at Lowfield with his locally-born wife Ellen and two servants.[69] His business is Spurr & Hunter's Barnes Colliery at Stubley in Dronfield parish, just over the Derbyshire border. Shortly after this he moves to upmarket Broomhill Terrace,[70] further up the hill from Leavy Greave where Sarah once had her school. In 1871 and 1881 Henry is in Southampton, living in some style on his dividend income with Ellen and again two servants. He dies there in 1884.[71]

And was Anthony H. Drury the British-born Russian Army officer, Captain Drury, who had been arrested and gaoled a few years earlier for circulating Knill's Testaments and tracts? The story is told of how after his release a General introduced him to other officers as 'the first officer of our army who was ever imprisoned for doing good'.[72]

William Ropes, a prosperous American, and members of his family also signed the petition. He had brought them to St Petersburg in 1832; at the house he had rented the Gellibrands had tea waiting for them.[73] Now, after a period working on commission, he had just set up his own import-export business, later employing Archibald Mirrielees for five years.[74] On Monday evenings the Ropes would host meetings for prayer and Tract Society business, with a tea-break between them.[75] William's eldest daughter Mary Tyler Ropes became William Gellibrand's second wife and his eldest son William Hooper Ropes married a niece of the first Mrs Gellibrand.[76] It was a tightly-knit community.

Briefly to complete the story of the chapel-building project: Richard Knill, as Sarah and her friends had rightly feared, did not come back. He missioned and ministered in various parts of the British Isles, finally settling in Chester where he died in 1857.[77] The missionary John Crombie Brown arrived in St Petersburg in the autumn of 1833 to take charge of the congregation, temporarily at first as he was intended for Siberia but in his own right from November 1835 after ordination. A minority objected to the appointment and left the congregation. The Rev Edward

Stallybrass, who ordained him with the assistance of the Moravian pastor Nielson, reported all this to London. He also implied dissatisfaction with the slow progress of the fund-raising which Richard had undertaken. With a target of £1000, only £300 had been collected.[78]

In 1836-37 John Brown made a visit to America and England, partly for that purpose, though he was disappointed with the results. A letter from his temporary replacement sheds further light on the need for a new chapel. The requirements of the host congregation meant that the visitors could not begin their first Sunday service until 12.30pm and there was no adequate opportunity to cool and ventilate the building. He evidently thought that the awkward time and the uncomfortable conditions militated against attracting a larger respectable congregation.[79] So they had to raise more funds themselves. William Ropes and his son starred in that role. The new building, officially called the British & American Congregational Church – not quite as had been predicted – and popularly known as the Chapel, was formally opened on 24 August 1840.[80] It was situated in Novo-Iskievskaya Street, only a short distance from its Anglican counterpart on the south quay of the Neva.[81] A new minister, Thomas Ellerby, had replaced John Brown in the previous year.

Literary Activities and Widowhood

Returning now to Sarah's personal doings, we may recall that the abolition of slavery had been a cause dear to Hannah Kilham's heart and that she passed on this interest to her stepdaughter. Although Parliament had abolished the trade in 1807 it was not until 1834 that the institution itself was outlawed in Britain's colonies. On 16 September of that year John Jackson wrote to her about the Society's £20,000 appeal towards meeting the spiritual needs of the liberated slaves. (It was popularly known as the Negro Fund.) Hannah had died 18 months earlier. Now Sarah called her to witness in her reply. 'How would her heart have rejoiced to see the dawn of the 1st of August!' When reading her journal 'our affections are almost involuntarily drawn out to that injured people, & the heart sometimes inexpressibly swells with the recital of their woes'. She offered a subscription of £10, asking for it to be listed as 'A tribute of affection to the memory of Hannah Kilham'. Jackson called it a 'handsome' contribution (its purchasing power in 2008 would be nearly £800). Eighteen months later she donated a further £5, to be recorded thus: 'From interest of money left by Hannah Kilham'.[82]

But for hindsight we might have been a little surprised to learn that one of Sarah's chief pursuits in the mid- to late 1830s was literary activity. She had inherited various papers from her stepmother, both Hannah's and some of Alexander's. After financial bequests, Hannah left Sarah the residue of her property, but did not say what this was.[83] Sarah received what she called a 'voluminous journal' but, it would seem, not much else.

At least, when editing the journal she alluded to a 'paucity' of other information, even after consulting friends. She suggested that this was partly due to the 'retired spirit' of Hannah, 'who always preferred that what she did should be little known, and still less the subject of conversation'.[84] Any of Sarah's Russian friends, reading this later, might well have recalled their proverb 'The apple doesn't fall far from the tree', forgetting that Hannah and Sarah were not blood relations. So Hannah became and has remained a good deal better known than Sarah, and it is Sarah whom we have to thank for this.

Sarah made copious extracts from Hannah's manuscript journal and linked them together with a substantial editorial commentary, adding an appendix by Hannah's sister and a tribute from James Montgomery, the Sheffield newspaper editor, reformer and poet. It is very likely indeed that the sister was Sarah Corbett, since the two had been very close and we know of no other sister with whom our Sarah was in touch. (Still in Liverpool, the Corbetts returned to Manchester in 1838. Matthew died in 1847. A year later his widow followed him and was buried at Mount Street.)[85] Montgomery wrote of Hannah: 'She was one of the most actively and influentially benevolent persons with whom it was ever my privilege to be acquainted'. In a poem dedicated to her memory he had called her 'dear saint'.[86]

MEMOIR
OF THE LATE
HANNAH KILHAM;
CHIEFLY COMPILED FROM
HER JOURNAL,
AND EDITED BY
HER DAUGHTER-IN-LAW
SARAH BILLER,
OF ST. PETERSBURG...
LONDON,
DARTON AND HARVEY,
GRACECHURCH-STREET.
1837

Sarah finished working on the *Memoir* on 4 April 1836. 'The selection has been made with increasing interest', she wrote, 'and no regret was felt till the close obliged us to take leave of a character so full of instruction and encouragement'. Now, however, regret had yielded to the hope that

Hannah's example might inspire many to wait on the Lord and do his will. (Sarah put this much less baldly.)[87] The book appeared the following year. 'Daughter-in-law', describing the editor on the title page, was commonly used about this time with the meaning of stepdaughter. One feels, incidentally, that Sarah, modest though she usually was, quite relished being 'Sarah Biller of St. Petersburg' and wanted to be known as such. So we are happy to indulge her.

Sarah's other literary activity at this time was by proxy: making her father's papers, as we have noted, available to John Blackwell for his unrivalled biography of the New Connexion founder. E.A. Rose made a rueful comment on this: 'Having survived a journey to St Petersburg and back in the 1830s, it is sad to reflect that some of these letters were lost in Sheffield a hundred years later!'[88] The reference to Sheffield is an allusion to a precarious stage in the travels of a substantial collection of Methodist printed and handwritten materials including Kilham correspondence and known as the Hobill Library, after the collector, G.A.K. Hobill. With Alexander Kilham as his two middle names, he must surely have felt a burden of care.

The letters were not the only loss. Whether in St Petersburg or somewhere else, Hannah's manuscript journal also went astray, so that we are unlikely ever to know how delicately Sarah went about her editorial task. True, she arranged for edited excerpts from the journal to be published a few years later, with the help of Hannah's friend John Reynolds, on the spot in Hampstead. *A Brook by the Way* (1844) – the title comes from the last verse of Psalm 110 – is a small book consisting of reflections from various points in Hannah's life, rather jumbled, with an appendix of letters. There is much overlapping with the *Memoir* but this time no reference at all to Sarah herself.[89] We can picture her sitting at her table in St Petersburg, back in self-effacing mode and deftly wielding the editorial scissors.

Late in 1837 or early in 1838, after six years of marriage, William Biller died. Of the circumstances we know nothing. The approximate date is deduced from a letter from John Jackson in London to John Brown in St Petersburg, mentioning that the Bible Society head office had already had news of the death of 'our good friend Mr Biller', and asking him to pass on their condolences to the widow.[90] No correspondence of Sarah's referring to her loss has come to light. The event is not recorded in the Anglican registers, nor would we expect it. William was probably buried according to the rites of the Lutheran Church from which he came and among whose St Petersburg members he appears to have had some family.

With Sarah soon accomplishing two decades of her life in the Russian capital and reaching her fiftieth birthday, it seems fitting that the completion of the middle stage of her career at St Petersburg should be marked by a letter to the man who had played a key role in bringing her there in the first place, William Allen. Back in 1819 after visiting St Petersburg and Moscow Allen and Stephen Grellet had travelled to the south of the Empire, including a stop in Ekaterinoslav (later Dnepropetrovsk), Ukraine. There they had met the saintly Archimandrite (Abbot) Makary or Makarius, a 'starets' (holy man, literally elder).[91] He was in fact one of the most distinguished elders of his generation, a scholarly man who finds a place in Timothy Ware's introduction to the Orthodox Church.[92] Twenty years later Sarah became acquainted with him and invited him to call at her school. This he did, writing to Allen a letter of blessings, which prompted her to send a covering letter telling him more about Makary and his visit.

Makary had talked about his mission of some years' duration to the Tobolsk area of Western Siberia and his wish to extend it by having women teach other women and girls in schools and families. Sarah would have encouraged him in this. He also spoke of his efforts to translate most of the Old Testament from Hebrew into Russian so that his compatriots could have the whole Bible in their mother tongue, but the leading clergy gave him no support. This was a familiar story, and Sarah with her Bible Society connections and experience was able to sympathize with him completely. But what impressed her most of all was his suggestion that they should read from the Scriptures – John 16:33 to 17:26, where Jesus prays for his disciples and for future believers – and then pray together, including the subject of the whole Bible for Russia, silently. Sarah was deeply impressed by this because it was quite extraordinary for an Orthodox priest to ask for silent prayer.[93] This would naturally have been of great interest to the Quaker William Allen, but it is interesting for us too, for clearly Sarah herself was still not fully severed from the Quaker stock on which the Methodist scion had been grafted so long ago.

Notes and References

1   CWM, Russia, RK's Journal, p 326.
2   SK, *NMM*, 33 (1830), p 278.
3   D.P. Runich, 'Iz zapisok D.P. Runicha', *Russkaya starina*, 106 (1901), pp 380, 394.
4   Birrell, p 105.
5   M.L. Magnitsky, 'O vodvorenii illyuminatstva pod raznymi ego vidami v Rossii', *Russkaya starina*, 97 (1899), p 303.
6   A. Stott, *Hannah More: The First Victorian* (Oxford, 2003), pp 213, 230-1, 245.
7   Magnitsky, p 306. He also cites a strange hybrid called the 'London Methodist Missionary Society' – the LMS in Methodist clothing? – as funder of the RBS.
8   Ibid., p 308.

9 Ibid., pp 312-3.

10 SK, *NMM*, 35 (1832), pp 81, 82.

11 'Velikaya knyaginya Elena Pavlovna, 1806-1873', *Russkaya starina*, 33 (1882), p 783.

12 Saunders, pp 209, 219-20.

13 L. Debono, 'La médecine en Russie de 1801 à 1917' (MD thesis, Université de Franche-Comté, 1997), pp 103-4.

14 SK, *NMM*, 35 (1832), pp 81-2.

15 CWM, Russia, In. Corr., 2/4/A, RK to W.A. Hankey, 26 June NS and 20 July OS 1831; Pitcher, pp 14-15.

16 SK, *NMM*, 33 (1830), p 278.

17 SK, *NMM*, 35 (1832), p 82.

18 K.-H. Günther *et al.*, *Geschichte der Erziehung* ([East] Berlin, 1987), pp 254-5.

19 BSA/D1/2/47, SB to John Jackson (hereafter JJ), 24 July 1834.

20 SB to WA, 22 June 1839, in *Allen*, 3, p 310.

21 Ibid.

22 SB to JV, 18 Oct 1841, in Henderson, pp 231-2.

23 BSA/D1/2/36, SK to JJ, 24 Oct 1831; cp. BSA/D1/2/41, William Biller (hereafter WB) to JJ, 4 Feb 1833.

24 GLL: St Petersburg Registers, Ms 11,194/1, Part II, p 157. For rival spellings of Mirrielees see Pitcher, pp 1-2.

25 Sykes, p 57.

26 Pitcher, pp 16-17.

27 Scott, p 94.

28 Greenwood, 2, p 145; neither he nor Scott appears to have picked up the register entry.

29 BSA/D1/2/47, WB to JJ, 24 July 1834.

30 *Rukovodstvo k otyskivaniyu zhilishch po Sanktpeterburgu* (St Petersburg, 1824), p 35.

31 BSA/D1/2/41, WB to JJ, 4 Feb 1833, and same to same: BSA/D1/2/47, 24 July 1834; BSA/D1/2/48, 13 Oct 1834; BSA/D1/2/53, 20 Mar 1836.

32 Ibid., last item.

33 Dr Hermann Beyer-Thoma, Osteuropa-Institut München, to the author, 6 Feb 2003.

34 CWM, Russia, RK's Journal, pp 230, 264, 315, 355.

35 CWM, Russia, In. Corr., 2/5/A, members to LMS, 5 June 1833.

36 BSA/D1/2/41, SB to JJ, 4 Feb 1833.

37 BSA/D1/2/48, WB to JJ, 13 Oct 1834 (copy at FHL: Temp Mss 212).

38 BSA/D1/2/48, SB to JJ, 13 Oct 1834.

39 BSA/D1/2/41, WB to JJ, 4 Feb 1833; his emphasis. 'At *a* throne of grace' may ring oddly to people conversant with Heb 4:16, but it was evidently a convention of the time. Sarah's grandmother had used it years earlier (MARC: Box 324 (2), Hannah Gray to HK, 27 Jan 1799), as did Jean Paterson, wife of John of the BFBS (Rosslyn, 'Women with a Mission', p 224).

40 BSA/D1/2/36, SK to JJ, 24 Oct 1831.

41 Information from Dr Julia Mahnke-Devlin, citing R. Steinberg, *Die Anfänge der Strafvollzugsreform in Rußland*... (Frankfurt am Main, 1990), p 167 ff; Henderson, pp 152-4.

42 As in A. Hamm, *Der heilige Doktor von Moskau* (Berlin and Bonn, 1979) and L. Kopelew, *Der heilige Doktor Fjodor Petrowitsch: die Geschichte des Friedrich Joseph Haass* (Hamburg, 1984). The Billers spelt his name with a single 's', but his German biographers invariably use two.

43 Hamm, pp 129-33; H. Müller-Dietz, *Friedrich Joseph Haass als Arzt in Moskau* (Berlin, 1980), pp 114-16.

44 Rosslyn, 'Benevolent Ladies', p 74.

45 BSA/D1/4/1/21 (23), JJ to SB, 21 Jan 1833; BSA/D1/2/41, WB to JJ, 4 Feb 1833; BSA/D1/2/42, SB to J.S. Reynolds, 15 Mar 1833.

46 BSA/D1/4/1/21 (237), JJ to SB, 31 May 1833; BSA/D1/2/47, WB to JJ, 24 July 1834; *Report of the BFBS*, 30 (1834), p xlvi.

47 BSA/D1/2/53, WB to JJ, 20 Mar 1836.

48 BSA/D1/2/48, SB to JJ, 13 Oct 1834.

49 *Istoricheskii ocherk Svyato-Troitskoi Obshchiny sestër miloserdiya v S.-Peterburge za pyatidesyatiletie 1844-1894* (St Petersburg, 1894), p 18.

50 BSA/D1/2/48, SB to JJ, 13 Oct 1834 O.S.

51 Henderson, pp 299-302.

52 *Istoricheskii ocherk*, p 18.

53 BSA/D1/2/36, SK to JJ, 24 Oct 1831 and *Report of the BFBS*, 28 (1832), p xlvii (the peasant); BSA/D1/2/41, SB to JJ, 4 Feb 1833 (Camidge and the salesman); BSA/D1/2/53, SB to JJ, 20 Mar 1836 (the clerk).

54 For more on the Molokans and a later description (1874), see R.S. Latimer, *Russia under Three Tsars* (Kilmarnock, n.d.), pp 37-42.

55 SB, copy of ms. of 8 Nov 1835 in Dublin Friends' archives, quoted in Greenwood, 1, pp 101-2.

56 Ibid.

57 BSA/D1/2/41, SB to JJ, 4 Feb 1833.

58 BSA/D1/2/53, SB to JJ, 20 Mar 1836.

59 BSA/D1/2/48, SB to JJ, 13 Oct 1834.

60 BSA/D1/2/41, SB to JJ, 4 Feb 1833; BSA/D1/2/48, SB to JJ, 13 Oct 1834. The family is described in 'Velikaya knyaginya', p 784.

61 *Report of the LMS*, 39 (1833), p 68.

62 Pitcher, p 15.

63 CWM, Russia, In. Corr., 2/5/A, RK to Thomas Wilson, 16 May 1833.

64 Birrell, p 190.

65 CWM, India & Russia, Out. Corr., William Ellis to RK, 22 May 1833; Russia, In. Corr., 2/5/A, members to LMS, 5 June 1833.

66 CWM, Russia, In. Corr., 2/5/A, RK to William Ellis, 6/18 June 1833, and to Thomas Wilson, 15 June.

67 Birrell, p 190.

68 FHL: Gibson IV/109, HK to [Mrs] Thomas Thompson, 6 Sep 1825; her emphasis.

69 Census returns, from: www.ancestrylibrary.com

70 White's *Directory of Sheffield*, various dates from 1849 to 1860.

71 Death index, from: www.ancestrylibrary.com

72 Birrell, pp 170-1.
73 Livingston, p 58.
74 Pitcher, p 18.
75 Livingston, p 58.
76 Ibid., p 57; Pitcher, pp 17, 34.
77 Birrell, pp 195-242.
78 CWM, Russia, In. Corr., 2/5/A, J.C. Brown to W. Ellis, 1 Oct 1833; 3/1/A, same to same, 11/23 Dec 1835, and E. Stallybrass to Ellis, 28 Nov/10 Dec 1835.
79 CWM, Russia, In. Corr., 3/1/C, J.C. Brown to Ellis, 10 June 1837, and J. Hands to Ellis, 24 Apr 1837.
80 Pitcher, p 15.
81 Grech, p 52.
82 BSA/D1/4/1/24, JJ to SB, 16 Sept and 20 Nov 1834; BSA/D1/2/48, SB to JJ, 13 Oct 1834; BSA/D1/2/53, SB to JJ, 20 Mar 1836.
83 TNA: Prob 11/1810, f 262.
84 Biller, ed., p i.
85 MCL: M85/2/6/1, p 151; M85/2/8, pp 77, 192.
86 Holland and Everett, 5, note to p 158.
87 Biller, ed., p i.
88 Rose, 'Sarah Kilham', p 186.
89 H. Kilham, *A Brook by the Way: Extracts from the Diary of Hannah Kilham* (London, 1844).
90 BSA/D1/4/1/32, JJ to J.C. Brown, 20 Feb 1838.
91 F. Wilson (p 207) points out that very little was known of these holy men in Western Europe until Dostoevsky's *The Brothers Karamazov* (1879-80) reached a wider public with its portrait of Father Zosima.
92 T. Ware, *The Orthodox Church* (Harmondsworth, 1963), p 133. Makary, he says, is one of the contenders for the inspiration of Dostoevsky's holy man.
93 Allen, 3, pp 309-10.

6. WORKING TILL NIGHTFALL

SARAH'S THIRD RUSSIAN DECADE

Directories and Directorships

OVER THE last of the three stages of Sarah Biller's time in Russia, she appears to have taken on a number of new and responsible tasks in addition to running the school. Past her fiftieth birthday, she seemingly felt that there was much to do and little time in which to do it, and therefore she should devote all her energy and talents to that end. As a firm Christian she followed Christ's pattern. The allusion in the chapter title is to John 9:4, in the version familiar to her: 'I must work the works of him that sent me, while it is day; the night cometh, when no man can work'.

Through the rest of Sarah's life there are sparse but compelling indications that she valued and wished to safeguard her somewhat tenuous links with the Society of Friends. John Venning was not a Quaker but, now settled in Norwich, had Quaker connections, notably with Amelia Opie, the once radically-minded novelist and poet who had joined the Friends in 1825, and Joseph John Gurney, the evangelical banker, philanthropist, prison reformer – his sister was Elizabeth Fry – and abolitionist. Writing to Venning in 1841, Sarah asked him to thank Gurney for the religious books which he had so kindly sent and which she had distributed 'among the high nobility'; he was, she said, a man she almost venerated. She also wanted him to remember her to Mrs Opie, 'whom, unknown personally, I love', and who had loved her 'mother' Hannah. She rejoiced that Mrs Opie now laboured for the Lord; she called it a happy change,[1] in unspoken recall of the distant days when Amelia had consorted with other radicals like the long-dead Mary Wollstonecraft Godwin and theatre people like the late Sarah Siddons.

Sarah also gave news of their one-time mutual Russian friends, with whom she was evidently still in touch. Princess Meshcherskaya, writing to her with an evangelical stress on her own unworthiness and unproductivity, invalidated the point by forwarding her translations of two small books.[2] As early as 1833 Robert Pinkerton had estimated that she had translated no fewer than 93 English tracts and other religious writings, publishing them primarily at her own expense.[3] 'Dear Prince Galitzin', Sarah added, 'is nearly blind, but full of love, peace and devotedness to the will of his heavenly Father'.[4] Since the abolition of Golitsyn's ministerial post and his ejection from the chair of the Russian Bible Society, both in 1824, he had held a number of uninfluential court positions, and it was failing eyesight that made him retire. He went to live in the Crimea in 1842 and died there in 1844, aged about 71.[5]

On just one occasion in the 1840s Sarah was witness to a marriage, but it is something of a puzzle since none of the names are familiar. It was at the English Church on 11 February O.S. 1843. The couple were John Roper (*not* Ropes), bachelor, and Mary Compton, spinster, once again described by the Rev Edward Law as 'of this congregation'. The other witnesses were Thomas Coulson and Mary Rushforth.[6] Either bride or groom or both of them must have been among Sarah's friends, probably at the new British and American Chapel if Mr Law was still regarding all St Petersburg as his parish. He, by the way, soldiered on at the English Church until 1864, sitting for his portrait by Timoléon Karl Neff, Court Painter, and then retired to Barnes in Surrey.[7]

Sarah's school continued, and she edited and published her step-mother's journal, but the 1840s were the decade *par excellence* when she expanded her professional activities. To take the school first, this is the time when it makes its belated début in two unusually close appearances of the rather infrequent city directories, published in 1849 and 1851. The 1849 entry, cited earlier, is in the section 'Girls' Schools': 'Lancasterian (of Mutual Instruction) for the Poor'.[8] As we have seen, the location can be pinpointed quite closely in the west end of the city, near and to the north-east of the principal mouth of the River Neva. Admittedly Sarah's name is not given, but we know of no other school that fits this description.

The 1851 appearance, in a directory compiled by A. Grech whose father and publisher had pioneered Lancasterian schools and who ought therefore to be reliable, is a little fuller, with two items in different parts of the work. The earlier item lists the school as an establishment under the patronage of the Grand Duchess Elena Pavlovna: 'Girls' School of Mutual Instruction, in Officers' Street [Ofitserskaya ulitsa], at Sukharny Bridge [most]. Director: Sarra Alexandrovna Biler'.[9] Sarra is the Russian form of Sarah according to its first occurrence in Genesis 17:15 as the new name of Abraham's wife. The later item spells Sarah's surname cor-rectly and adds the school's exact address: Stepanov (or Stepanov's) House.[10] This is different from two years previously (St Michael's Church House) and seems to indicate a re-location within the same area. The Sukharny Bridge, now gone, was in fact the westernmost one over the Moika, just north-east of its junction with the Pryazhka and a block away from Officers' Street.[11]

The first item in the 1851 directory includes a little more information which should be useful for anyone inclined to delve into the administra-tive history of Sarah's school. It came within the purview of the Main

Board of Female Educational Establishments *(Glavnyi sovet zhenskikh uchebnykh zavedenii)* in the Office of the Institutions of the Empress Maria *(Vedomstvo uchrezhdenii Imperatritsy Marii)*.[12] This body's remit can be traced back to 1796 when the Emperor Paul put his wife in overall charge of the Society for the Upbringing of Girls of Noble Birth (the Smolny Institute), and through 1826 when Nicholas I divided his Chancellery into four departments, the fourth of which administered philanthropic and educational institutions.[13] When exactly Sarah's school was transferred to this from the Department of the State Economy and Public Buildings – a location which we have not seen confirmed but which is implied by Privy Councillor S.S. Dzhunkovsky's role as its superintendent in 1825 – is unclear. It must, however, have been at some point after the Empress Maria died in 1828, as the school does not figure in a list of her educational and charitable institutions founded between 1797 and that year.[14] Perhaps the change occurred in 1831, when Dzhunkovsky was again reported to be in command of the 'Quaker-run' schools[15] but the Emperor's sister-in-law became the patron of Sarah's.

It is interesting that Sarah was explicitly stated to be the director of this school in 1851. In fact it is more than interesting, it is bizarre, but we must wait a little to see why. Russian sources raise a minor problem and a major one. Let us first address the minor one, next consider the background and scope of an enormous change in her career, and then discuss the difficulty that this presents.

The State Historical Archive contains a file on the Benevolent Society of English Ladies at St Petersburg, founded in 1841 by six of them including Mrs Mary Gellibrand and Mrs Law, wife of the Anglican Chaplain, to help poor foreigners from private donations (except their British compatriots who, they said, were assisted by the English Factory). Early in 1843 they applied to the Emperor Nicholas for financial support,[16] and this led his officials to draw up a list of charitable and philanthropic institutions to which he already contributed. The document contains two references to the Magdalen Institution founded at St Petersburg by 'the Quakeress Biller' on 22 April 1842. It was to receive 1000 roubles' worth of imperial aid each year.[17] (As for the Benevolent Ladies, they were awarded 500 roubles a year from February 1843.)[18] The question is: how does this relate to the Magdalen of 1833? Nowhere is there any reference to Sarah founding or co-founding *two* such institutions. The most likely explanation is that the 1842 Magdalen was some kind of re-foundation of the earlier one.

We may also note that, however difficult it might have been for Sarah in her Russian isolation to be a practising member of the Society of Friends, she was still very much associated with the Quakers in the eyes of the imperial authorities. This connection was soon reinforced by a further undertaking in the Quaker philanthropic tradition. Compared with her school, this has received minuscule attention in English accounts of her doings. Richenda Scott makes a passing (and misleading) reference to it: 'The Emperor, Nicholas I, held her in such high regard that he built a hospital in 1844 to be under her management and direction. She died in 1852, and her hospital passed into the care of the Sisters of Charity'.[19] Ormerod Greenwood phrases it differently and, as Russian accounts will show, a little more accurately: 'In 1844 Sarah Biller was able to open, under Imperial patronage, the first Hospital for Women in the Russian capital... Her hospital was continued by the "Sisters of Charity"'.[20] As we shall see, among Quaker visitors to St Petersburg the memory was to live on. But a history published to mark the fiftieth anniversary of the order[21] and Russian websites combine to tell a different story.

The truth of the matter is that both these quotations put the cart before the horse and do not reveal what a versatile thoroughbred the horse was. (To compare a nursing order to a horse may be thought odd, but a little later Sarah would certainly crack the whip.) First we must go back a few years and bring in a new character. On 11 April 1837 Prince P.G.

Community of Sisters of Charity, St Petersburg, 1844.

Ol'denburgsky, otherwise Prince Peter of Oldenburg, married the 22-year-old Princess Theresa of Nassau. Oldenburg and Nassau were originally German duchies and the Oldenburgs were closely connected with the Russian imperial family. Princess Theresa shared an interest with Sarah: in 1841 she took charge of a school for poor girls which her philanthropically-minded husband had recently set up on Petrograd Side, the big island area north-east of Vasil'evsky Island and north of the Peter and Paul Fortress.[22]

Two years later the Princess encountered the Community of Sisters of Charity when visiting a children's hospital which they ran in Warsaw.[23] This evidently prompted her to take a lead in founding Russia's first Orthodox Community of Sisters of Charity in St Petersburg on 9 March 1844. She enlisted the help of Grand Duchess Alexandra Nikolaevna, the Emperor's third daughter, in financing the project. The society of up to 30 Sisters and 20 probationers took part in an impressive range of charitable activities, based in originally rented premises in the Rozhdestvensky quarter of the city, and Nicholas installed a chapel dedicated to the Holy Trinity.[24] The locality feels tucked away but is in fact immediately northeast of the present-day Uprising Square (ploshchad' Vosstaniya) and Moscow Station. The site lay between today's 2nd Soviet Street and 3rd Soviet Street, or 2-ya (vtoraya) and 3-ya (tret'ya) Sovetskaya, then called Rozhdestvenskaya.

The institutions of the Community of Sisters of Charity were sixfold. First and uniquely famous in earlier accounts of Sarah was its Women's Hospital with 25 beds. A kind of almshouse for incurables offered another six beds. Then there was a 'Department of Penitent Magdalens', or 'Penitents' Department' for short; we referred to this type of home just now and will shortly do so again. The other three departments were concerned with child welfare and education. One was a school for maladjusted youngsters with 20 places. Another was a 'priyut', a shelter or centre for street children. The third, intriguingly, was a boarding school for poor girls, which also prompts speculation. The latter two shared the same wing as the Community director's apartment and a Lutheran chapel.[25] It now becomes understandable why Sarah, a few years later in England, would allow herself to be described as 'Directress of the Institutions'.[26] But before considering the boarding school and the Magdalens, can any more light be shed on how she acquired this complicated role?

Contrary to previous reports, Sarah was not formally in charge of the hospital from the outset. Just a few weeks after the founding of the Community of Sisters of Charity, the Grand Duchess Alexandra Nikolaevna, still in her late teens, died in childbirth.[27] The Empress Alexandra Fyodorovna thereupon assumed the patronage of the Community in honour of her daughter. A committee of management was set up, headed by the dead woman's eldest sister, the Grand Duchess Maria Nikolaevna and Princess Theresa of Oldenburg, and otherwise consisting of three princesses, four countesses and five ladies including Sarah Biller. Although members did duty in turn, urgent matters were handled by Sarah with the help of the doctor and the priest. Day-to-day management by committee was not practical and we can see which way the wind was blowing. Two years later, in 1846, Maria Nikolaevna became the governor of the Community and it was not until then that Sarah was installed as its director.[28]

Listing the city's hospitals, the 1851 directory gives pride of place to the 'Grand Duchess Alexandra Nikolaevna Memorial Hospital' and describes it as a constituent part of the Community of Sisters of Charity but under the same authority as the Mariinskaya Hospital, the big hospital for the poor on Liteiny prospekt a few blocks to the west, built in 1803 with the support of the Empress Mother.[29] This wider authority presumably implies medical services first and foremost. Be that as it may, the story that Nicholas I built the hospital for Sarah to run is pure fiction. It was, however, 'under Imperial patronage' in the persons of the Emperor's daughters and wife, and after Sarah left it was indeed 'continued by the Sisters of Charity' because they had been there from the start. Greenwood was either a canny historian or a lucky one.

Community of Sisters of Charity: Pharmacy and Dressings Room 1844.

Russian sources certainly help to clarify Sarah's role in the management of the Sisters of Charity and their hospital. They also support our suggestion about the minor problem of the Magdalens: we are told that the 'Penitents' Department' was an incorporation of the Magdalen refuge founded by Sarah and A.F. Mikhel'son. In fact the historian of the Sisters of Charity asserts that this was one of two conditions Sarah successfully laid down when the Grand Duchess Maria and Princess Theresa originally asked her to take part in their planned Community.[30] Thulia Henderson also sees continuity from the 1830s: 'To this day [1862] the Magdalen has survived; *not* however as an isolated establishment, but as a branch of a large charitable institution under the patronage of one of the Grand Duchesses'.[31]

And what of the major problem? At a late stage of writing this book it came as a surprise to read that the Sisters' boarding school for poor girls had been re-organized in 1844 from Sarah's original school of 1821. This had been her second condition for participating in the project.[32] It was quite unexpected because of the detailed references to her school, noted earlier, in Grech's directory published in 1851 and its predecessor. The re-organization of 1844 could not have been temporary, thus earning the school a different address seven years later, because it remained part of the Community until 1885 when the decision was taken to concentrate on helping the sick and to wind up all the Sisters' other activities.[33] Since we know that Sarah's earlier school gradually became popular with day pupils also, it is just possible that it had split into two and the one listed by Grech was the day school. Nowhere is there any hint of this, however, and one certainly hopes that it was not so, for then poor Sarah would have had two schools to run on top of everything else in the Community. The alternative explanation, unlikely though it may seem, is that in this instance Grech was seven years behind the times.

Once incorporated into the Community, the school was known initially as the Boarding School (pansion) and later as the Pupils' Department. Its aim was to provide care and elementary education for girls of 6 to 13. They included orphans, the daughters of poor parents and those of parents prevented by circumstances from bringing them up properly. Over the 40 years of the school's further existence, we are told, it did not undergo any noteworthy changes.[34]

Russian evaluations of Sarah are hard to find, so an exception to the rule is worth quoting:

> Her energy and assiduity were amazing. She was the first to get up and the last to go to bed. Not a single area of the work would she hand over to anyone else. Her persistence in pursuit of a set goal and her requirement of strict discipline among her subordinates

were justified in everyone's eyes by her personal example and that spirit of Christian gentleness which permeated all her relationships. She never permitted herself a sharp word, she never raised her voice, and everyone in the Community obeyed her unconditionally and without complaint... Sarra Alexandrovna had complete respect for the teachings and ceremonies of the Orthodox Church and attached particular importance to building people up in the word of God. On Sundays, therefore, she gathered together the Sisters, children and servants in the Community and herself read to them in Russian and expounded the Gospel.[35]

This verbal portrait of the strong-minded, self-controlled and rather austere woman is mirrored in the one by the artist.

Before looking at the hospital's later contacts with Quakers, let us sketch out the rest of the story of the Sisters and their activities. Early in the 1850s, as we shall see, Sarah left for England, and the lack of her firm hand seems to have affected the Community. Its household management and its discipline fell into such disarray that the question of closure arose.[36] In 1853 the street children's centre and the school for maladjusted youngsters were indeed discontinued. Two years later admission to the order was restricted to Orthodox women and the Lutheran chapel was closed, though we do not know what lay behind this.

From 1859, however, when a new director, E.A. Kublitskaya, took charge, the Community enjoyed a renaissance. The buildings soon saw the first of several extensions. In 1863 the organization of the Community was somewhat streamlined as the Department of Penitent Magdalens regained its independence and the little almshouse for incurables became an annexe for elderly and infirm Sisters. When major reconstruction took place a decade later and the Orthodox Chapel of the Holy Trinity was moved and refurbished, the society acquired the enlarged title of Community of Sisters of Charity of the Holy Trinity. Two other phases of building and rebuilding followed. In line with the decision of 1885, nine years later all 48 Sisters were engaged in hospital or related work, including home visits. Throughout the Community's existence, the Oldenburg family provided funding and leadership. After the October Revolution of 1917, however, the nursing order was disbanded.[37]

Through the rest of the 19th century the Quaker links of the Alexandra Nikolaevna Memorial Hospital were periodically reasserted.[38] In 1858, during their rather unsuccessful trip to circulate a Quaker Plea for Liberty of Conscience, Robert Forster and Robert Charleton visited it, referring to it as 'an institution formerly superintended by Sarah Biller. Everything appeared in good order, and, as far as we could judge, efficiently managed; and we were quite pleased with our first visit to this interesting place'. They went armed with a letter of introduction to 'Marie Matouseevitch... at the "Sisters of Charity"'.[39] She had been with Sarah in England in 1851. Maria Stanislavovna Matusevich would still be at work in the hospital in her seventies, at the time of its 50th anniversary.[40]

In 1891 the Volga provinces of Russia were struck by a dreadful famine, the outcome of several poor harvests and drought, and the Friends responded. The Meeting for Sufferings (the standing committee of London Yearly Meeting) established an *ad hoc* committee to investigate the famine and, if appropriate, organize relief. The Essex engineer and linguist Edmund Wright Brooks, accompanied by Francis William Fox, went to Russia on a fact-finding mission. The ultimate result was that in 1892 the Friends Russian Famine Fund was set up, raising some £40,000 – say £3m in 2008 – and Brooks made a second visit to supervise the distribution of funds.[41]

An event quite incidental to this relief project is highly relevant to the story of Sarah. Newly back in England in January 1892, Francis William Fox had written his report to the Famine Relief Committee. Near the end of the report he went off at a tangent:

> It may be interesting to the Committee to know that I paid a visit to a Hospital, erected by the Emperor Nicholas in 1844, but organised and superintended by Sarah Biller, a Lady member of the Society of Friends, whose name and memory are still much beloved and revered by the Sisters of Mercy who are in charge of the Hospital... The Lady Superintendent, Madame Abasa, showed me over the Hospital, which is capable of holding 100 patients of both sexes.[42]

In 1884 a newly-built 50-bed hospital for men had been added to the complex.[43] Fox went on to trace Sarah's link, through Daniel Wheeler, with the Emperor Alexander, starting or perpetuating the legend that his successor Nicholas 'esteemed her so highly that he built the hospital for her to superintend'.[44] It may well have been thanks to this reminder from Fox that when the Russian Famine Fund was wound up in 1893 the unspent balance of £6 8s 7d – an apparently trifling sum but worth about £450 in 2008 terms[45] – was 'forwarded to the Hospital for Women in St Petersburg, which is associated with the name of Sarah Billar *(sic)*, and its receipt has been gratefully acknowledged'.[46]

In 1896 Edmund Wright Brooks was despatched to Russia yet again, this time in the company of his wife Lucy Ann and Hannah F. White, secretly to gather information from dissenting groups in St Petersburg on the persecution of the Dukhobor sect in the Caucasus. Whilst in the city the Brooks visited a hospital accommodating about 80 patients. It appeared to be well run and was no doubt the one just mentioned, but

Lucy Ann misleadingly commented that its first matron was 'an English friend Hannah Kilham'.[47] The Quaker association was still present, at least in the minds of the Brooks, but since they confused Sarah with her stepmother it is unsafe to cite this as evidence that the former was regarded as a lifelong Friend at this time.[48]

Unlike the religious order, the hospital survived the Revolution. The thread linking the imperial past of the site with our own day, however, is not hands-on care of the sick but medical research. In 1886 another of the Oldenburgs, Prince Alexander, set up and funded a centre for inoculation against rabies, and four years later this became the Imperial Institute of Experimental Medicine, the first such centre in Russia. Research continues here in 2009 at the Russian Institute of Haematology and Transfusiology. You will not be able to find the buildings familiar to Sarah, for a further programme of reconstruction, this time fundamental, was carried out around 1890. Nevertheless a visit to the Institute's front door at No. 16, 2nd Soviet Street or 2-ya Sovetskaya ulitsa will bring you as close as you can get, in your mind's eye, to her hospital, the Sisters' quarters and the Orthodox chapel. And to round it off, turn into Degtyarnaya Street alongside the block and then into 3-ya Sovetskaya, where at No. 13 by stretching your imagination a very long way you may visualize the boarding school, the centre for street children, the Lutheran chapel and the apartment of Sarah Biller herself.[49]

Two Friends of Sarah's

Before bringing Sarah's story to a close, let us take leave of her two best-known British friends in St Petersburg, William Gellibrand and Archibald Mirrielees. The former was probably the first to return to England, soon after February 1854 when he had been very helpful and hospitable to the Quaker deputation on their brave but fruitless mission as Christian peacemakers to avert the Crimean War.[50] He had reached his sixtieth birthday in 1851 but did not admit to retiring very willingly. After over two decades of the St Petersburg climate it seems that his American second wife Mary had finally had enough of it, but he wrote to a relative that he was sorry to leave. He felt at home in Russia and had 'no family and few friends in England'. Both his marriages had been childless.

For a year the Gellibrands rented Bradenham Hall in Norfolk from the novelist H. Rider Haggard's father. Mary's sister Louisa Ropes came to live with them. Then they moved to what was regarded as one of the stately homes of England, Albyns in the parish of Stapleford Abbotts north of Romford, Essex, costing William the princely annual sum of £5000 (rent £2000, maintenance £3000). In present-day terms he must have been a multi-millionaire to have afforded this. Nor does it seem to have imposed any brake on his philanthropic activities. He died in 1884, had a splendid funeral and was buried in the village churchyard.[51]

The 1830s were a sad time for Archibald Mirrielees. The death of his wife Sarah, Hannah Kilham's niece, was followed by those of his younger daughter Frances and in 1839 his second wife Mary. Two of Sarah's children survived: William, whose middle name recalled his mother's maiden name of Spurr, and Sarah Jane. In 1842 Archibald resigned his post at William Ropes & Co. and the next year founded his own business importing such products as cotton and lace. Also in 1843 he took the two children with their German governess, Miss Funck[52] – yet another friend of Sarah Kilham's[53] – on a lengthy visit to Britain.

In Edinburgh Archibald got to know Jane Muir, an old friend of his second wife, and ten months later they were married. She gave him six more children, five of whom survived infancy, and also provided him with a brother-in-law, Andrew Muir, who came into the firm in 1852. Five years later he took over the business in partnership with the eldest Mirrielees son William. Thus the famous firm Muir & Mirrielees was born, whose history is chronicled in Harvey Pitcher's eponymous book and whose palatial later store in Moscow near the Bolshoi Theatre retained its fame as TsUM (*Tsentral'nyi universal'nyi magazin,* Central Universal Store, not to be confused with GUM on Red Square).

With the establishment of the partnership Archibald and Jane returned after a period on the Continent to England, living at first in Slough and later in Ealing.[54] They had annual reunions with the Gellibrands at Albyns. Whilst in Russia Archibald had been very active on behalf of the British and Foreign Bible Society; indeed while Britain was engaged in the Crimean War (1854-56) he as a person trusted by the Russians was in charge of the Society's North Russian agency.[55] In a wider context, people who have heard about the internment of Germans in our own country during both World Wars will be amazed to hear that British residents in Russia underwent no restrictions in the Crimean War,[56] though some did choose to leave. Now in Archibald's retirement the BFBS became his main interest. He was appointed an Honorary Life Governor and Committee member, which entailed weekly visits to headquarters, and the Society marked his death in 1877 with a highly appreciative obituary.[57] He, Jane and their daughter Augusta are buried at Stoke Poges.[58]

Sarah's Last Years

The story of Sarah Biller's last few years must needs be quickly told. It would be no wonder if archival repositories in St Petersburg contained as yet undiscovered material on her professional activities after 1844, but it is rather surprising that the major English sources fall silent in that final decade. So, naturally abhorring a vacuum, we can only fill it with conjecture based on the sparse facts, relieved by a true story of how a would-be biographer made an assumption which was initially frustrated far away and finally made null and void close to home. It seems reasonable to assume that as Sarah grew older and more and more separated from her native land – there was no return visit to renew her links around 1840 – and as friends and relatives from older generations died with no new ones to replace them, she had less occasion to write letters. On top of that, with a school and a women's home to look after, and later an entire religious community including these two plus a hospital and three other institutions, she must have been extremely busy, probably busier than ever before. No wonder that four years of this would bring about a serious breakdown of her health.

That Sarah died in 1852 I first learned from Richenda Scott,[59] but that classic on Quaker doings in Russia makes no mention of how or where it happened. I assumed, therefore, that she had died in harness in St Petersburg, and on a visit to that city a long time ago I tracked down the cemetery for foreign Protestants, trusting in pure serendipity to lead me to her resting place and perhaps an enlightening inscription. When I arrived there, what I saw in the oncoming dusk was a dense and quite impenetrable mini-forest of small bushy trees, under which row after row of little white crosses soon vanished into darkness. Thus serendipity had no chance to do its work. In fact my plan was even more doomed from the outset than I thought.

Years later, returning to the subject of Sarah's vital records, I decided to explore the standard genealogical sources, and so discovered not only the hoped-for date and place of her baptism but also the wholly unexpected date and place of her burial: at Evesham in April 1852. An announcement of her death appeared in the two Quaker papers: 'THIRD MONTH. 29th – At Evesham, Worcestershire, SARAH BILLER, late of Petersburg, aged 63 years'.[60] There were, however, no obituaries. The local press, *Berrow's Worcester Journal* and the *Worcester Herald*, had nothing at all to say about her.

Sarah's death certificate told me more. The death was registered three days later in Evesham by Dr Anthony Martin, a local surgeon and GP, who had witnessed it. She had died in Evesham High Street, perhaps in the actual street, perhaps where she was staying, perhaps at the doctor's house there. At any event, she died in the arms of Maria Matusevich, her travelling companion and favourite former pupil. Her occupation was given as 'Widow of William Biller, Gentleman'; this evidence of his status confirms what we have long believed. The cause of her death was: 'Apoplexy 2 year ago. Paralysis since'.[61]

Apoplexy is a general term, now barely used, meaning disturbance of the brain's function due to interference with the circulation of blood to it. This results from conditions more familiar to us: cerebral thromboses, embolisms and aneurysms. Most common is thrombosis, blood coagulating in the brain and impeding the supply of oxygen. With embolism a small blood clot travels to the brain from another part of the body and again causes obstruction. Aneurism occurs when the walls of blood vessels are weakened and distended, potentially leading to haemorrhage and in turn nerve damage. Overwork is a common trigger of apoplexy, and outcomes include strokes, fits and paralysis. In 1850, at 61 and working till nightfall, Sarah had most likely had a thrombosis leading to an unknown degree of physical impairment, which may have temporarily improved. The certificate was less specific about the immediate cause of death on that day in March 1852. Probably the doctor's words implied a fatal recurrence of the old problem or something related to it.

Directories are conventionally assumed to have been produced from data available the year before their publication. Grech must have been compiling his 1851 directory around the time when Sarah had had her attack. But it was already out of date and increasingly so. Soon after this intimation of her mortality she decided to give up her responsibilities and return to her motherland.[62] Fortunately for her biographer, she was back in England in time for the census taken on the evening of 30 March 1851. She was staying at Miss Catharine Williams's boarding house at 11, South Parade, Bath, where she had perhaps gone to take the waters for her health. Miss Williams, the enumerator's informant, described her grandiloquently but vaguely as 'Directress of the Institutions, St Petersburgh, Russia'. As Sarah was neither grandiloquent nor vague, this must have been the landlady's take on what sounded an enormous and important job. It was still too much on Sarah's mind for her to give the impression that she had retired. As we know, she was accompanied by 'Mary Matouseevitch', described as a 30-year-old teacher,[63] who had no doubt been working at the Community's school.

How Sarah came to be in Evesham also remained obscure initially. We knew of no earlier connection with this place. Might she have been visiting friends or relations? As it turned out, Evesham still had a secret or two to yield up.

Notes and References

1   Henderson, p 232.
2   Ibid.
3   Rosslyn, 'Benevolent Ladies', p 69, citing R. Pinkerton, *Russia, or Miscellaneous Observations of the Past and Present State of that Country and its Inhabitants* (London, 1833), p 358.
4   Henderson, p 232.

5   Martin, p 201.
6   GLL: St Petersburg Registers, Ms 11,194/1, Part III, p 295.
7   LRA: Ms 1117/1-2. The portrait is in the Brotherton Library, University of Leeds.
8   *Gorodskoi ukazatel'*, p 451.
9   A. Grech, comp., *Ves' Peterburg v karmane* (St Petersburg, 1851), p 226.
10 Ibid., p 530; here the street is called Great Officers' Street.
11 V.V. Kukushkin, *Toponomika Peterburga-Petrograda...* (St Petersburg, 2000), p 256.
12 Grech, comp., p 226.
13 S.G. Pushkarev, *Obzor russkoi istorii* (New York, 1953), p 387; *Pedagogicheskaya entsiklopediya*, 1 (Moscow, 1964), col 303.
14 I.R. Fon-der-khoven, 'Pamyatnik imperatritse Marii Feodorovne', *Russkaya starina*, 9 (1874), pp 203-4.
15 Magnitsky, pp 312-13. The Quakers (i.e. the Wheelers) carrying out the land reclamation project were answerable to Dzhunkovsky; the Russian text here, which is loosely constructed, seems to mean that those running schools (Sarah and James Heard) still answered to him too.
16 RGIA: 1287/16/1195, ff 1-7.
17 Ibid., ff 8, 10; Mahnke-Devlin, p 221.
18 RGIA: 1287/16/1195, f 12.
19 Scott, p 94, probably relying on F.W. Fox (FHL: SR 323/3/11). The Russian 'Sestry miloserdiya' may be translated as either Sisters of Charity or Sisters of Mercy. In the West these are basically separate orders, the former Catholic, the latter Catholic or Protestant.
20 Greenwood, 2, p 145.
21 *Istoricheskii ocherk*, esp. pp 7, 18.
22 'Ol'denburgskaya   printsessa   Tereziya-Vil'gel'mina-Frederika-Izabella-Sharlotta', *Biografii Rossiiskikh uchenykh, politikov, literaturnykh deyatelei* (2007), from: www.inform-t.ru/show_bio.aspx_id_100548.php (accessed 13 Mar 2009).
23 'Svyato-Troitskaya obshchina sester miloserdiya – NII gematologii i trans-fuziologii' (2005), from: www.citywalls.ru/house3421.html (accessed 13 Mar 2009).
24 Ibid.; V.P. Romanyuk, V.A. Lapotnikov and Ya.A. Nakatis, 'Istoriya ses-trichestva i ukhoda za bol'nymi: 3. Obshchiny sester miloserdiya', *Zolotoi khorets* (2004), from: www.randd.ru/Miloserdie_3.htm (accessed 13 Mar 2009).
25 Conflated from lists in 'Svyato-Troitskaya obshchina' and Romanyuk *et al.*
26 Census returns, 1851, from: www.ancestrylibrary.com
27 L. Hughes, *The Romanovs: Ruling Russia, 1613-1917* (London, 2008), pp 164, 173.
28 *Istoricheskii ocherk*, p 7; 'Svyato-Troitskaya obshchina'.
29 Grech, comp., pp 39, 406; T.A. Schrader, 'Der Beitrag deutscher Ärzte zur Entwicklung der Krankenhäuser in St Petersburg im 19. Jahrhundert', in I. Kästner and R. Pfrepper, ed., *Medizin und Pharmazie im 18. und 19. Jahrhundert* (Aachen, 2000), p 136. I have used 'Memorial' to translate a Russian term meaning 'resting in God'.

30 *Istoricheskii ocherk*, p 18.
31 Henderson, pp 301-2; her emphasis.
32 *Istoricheskii ocherk*, pp 18, 64; 'Svyato-Troitskaya obshchina'.
33 Ibid.
34 *Istoricheskii ocherk*, p 64.
35 Ibid., p 19.
36 Romanyuk *et al.*
37 Ibid.; 'Svyato-Troitskaya obshchina'.
38 Scott, p 94; Greenwood, 2, p 145.
39 A.F. Fox, ed., *Memoir of Robert Charleton* (London, 1873), p 119; context in Scott, pp 101-3.
40 Census returns, from: www.ancestrylibrary.com; *Istoricheskii ocherk*, p 19.
41 For a full account of the project, see Scott, pp 130-6.
42 FHL: SR 323/3/11. Madame Abasa also told Fox that the last Friends to visit the hospital had been Joseph Sturge, Robert Charleton and Henry Pease in 1854 (during their attempt to avert the Crimean War), but such a visit is not mentioned in the story of their mission (G.F. Mason, *Sleigh Ride to Russia* (York, 1985)). If it indeed took place it was certainly not the most recent one.
43 Romanyuk *et al.*
44 FHL: SR 323/3/11.
45 Derived from rates for 2007 at www.measuringworth.com, accessed in 2008.
46 FHL: Meeting for Sufferings, Minutes, 1892 to 1896, p 233. The minute is dated 5th of 1st Month (5 Jan) 1894, not 1895 as cited by Greenwood, 2, p 298 n 35.
47 FHL: Temp Mss 592, Box 2, Edward Bernstein Papers, Lucy Ann Brooks, 'Russian Notes 1896', p 3; context in Scott, pp 137-8.
48 As Scott does, p 94 n 2, misquoting the Brooks notes.
49 Romanyuk *et al.*; 'Svyato-Troitskaya obshchina'.
50 Mason, pp 43, 46-7, 56-7, 60-1, 76, 85.
51 LRA: Ms 1110/4 (Bradenham Hall, not Brammerton as stated in the source).
52 Pitcher, pp 17-18, 39.
53 CWM, Russia, RK's Journal, p 270.
54 Pitcher, pp ix-x, 27, 40-1, 44, 52.
55 LRA: Ms 1193/1, *Bible Society Monthly Reporter*, 2 Apr 1877.
56 Pitcher, p 41.
57 LRA: Ms 1193/1.
58 Pitcher, p 56.
59 Scott, p 94.
60 *The Friend*, 10, 1852, no 112, p 78; also in *The British Friend*. Friends House Library is well-stocked with obituaries but Sarah's is not among them.
61 Evesham Registry Office, Copy of an Entry of Death, 15 Aug 2001 (original no. 181, 1852); for Maria, *Istoricheskii ocherk*, p 19.
62 Ibid.
63 Census returns, from: www.ancestrylibrary.com

7. REMEMBERING SARAH

JUST AROUND the corner from Evesham High Street, off Bridge Street, is Cowl Street. If you are in a hurry it is easy to miss the Friends' Meeting House. At a large black and white building flanking the street you go down a passageway and there it is, at the side of a charming garden which was once the burial ground. The meeting house began life in 1676 and what you see is an extensive rebuilding in brick – now rendered over and painted white – from 1698 with the burial ground added in 1721.[1] The lawn is partly covered by flat gravestones, nearly all from the second half of the 19th century. Also, praises be, there exists a detailed Victorian plan of the whole site.[2] Plot 64 has the name of Sarah Biller against it, and there is a stone. In the garden, passing the length of the meeting house on your right and turning at the gable end, you come to some bushes beside an ancient greenhouse. You may have to scrabble under the bushes to find the stone in the row closest to the meeting house, and then scatter salt and brush most of it away to make the engraved inscription plain. It simply reads:

> SARAH BILLER
> DIED
> 3 MO. 29 1852
> AGED
> 63 YEARS

If Sarah had died only a few years earlier, such a stone might well never have existed, for between 1717 and 1850 Quakers usually considered memorials to be idolatrous.

Nor is that quite all. To leave no stone unchecked, you may wish to go back to the plan; and there you find, on the plot closest to Sarah's, No. 80, the name of Elizabeth Corbett, who died in 1896. Here, you might well suppose, is a link with Hannah Kilham's niece and Sarah's one-time colleague, Ann Corbett, and Matthew of Pendleton with whom she stayed on her way to Southport in February 1831. You would be right. Elizabeth, one of Matthew's daughters, aged about 35 and living in Pimlott or Pimblett Street, Pendleton, in 1841, then disappeared from the census lists for three decades, eventually showing up at Altrincham. Then in 1881 and 1891 she was living on her own means and lodging at Jane Rodd's house, 32 High Street, Evesham.[3] What had brought her to that town remained at first as mysterious as what had brought Sarah there thirty years earlier.

Friends Meeting House, Evesham, in 2003.
Sarah's gravestone (below) is under the bushes at the gable end.

But then the Quaker records at Manchester Central Library came a long way to the rescue. Membership lists revealed that Elizabeth spent a year in the Worcester area from 1835 to 1836.[4] We do not know why, only that she was there. Next the spotlight focuses on Hannah Corbett, her Kilham namesake's favourite niece whom she committed in her will to Sarah's care. Transferring from Manchester to Southwark in 1831, young Hannah moved at some stage to Worcestershire, from where she returned to Pendleton for a few months in 1839 before marrying a certain H. Burlingham.[5] The Burlinghams were prominent members of Evesham Meeting. It was presumably the same Henry Burlingham who signed the 1851 religious census return for the Evesham Friends: 21 morning attenders, 14 in the afternoon.[6] The family lived at Lansdowne House, 42 Port Street, the main street of Bengeworth, the Evesham suburb east of the Avon. About the time of Sarah's last visit the household of ten included four young children and four servants, one of whom was their governess. Henry and Hannah had named their eldest Hannah Kilham Burlingham.[7] In Billing's *Directory of Worcestershire* (1855) Henry is described as an iron-monger, iron and coal dealer and wharfinger (owner or manager of a wharf).[8] Hannah and Henry Burlingham died at an advanced age in 1895 and 1896 respectively and were buried in an unusually large plot not far from Sarah's.[9] Clearly the Burlinghams were the magnet that drew their relations to Evesham.

The meeting house contains a library and here it was that I first came across the work of Ormerod Greenwood, a name well known to Quaker historians but apparently unfamiliar to others who have written on Russia. In *Quaker Encounters 2: Vines on the Mountains* (1977) he adds lively details of the activities and relationships of the persons in our drama to whom we were introduced by Jane Benson[10] or, from a much later generation, Richenda Scott. Greenwood actually gives the place and date of Sarah Biller's death. Had I seen his book sooner I should not have made my memorable wild goose chase across Leningrad, as it then was.

Quaker writers agree that, far from being disowned – which might have resulted from Daniel Wheeler's report of Sarah's move to Richard Knill's congregation – she remained a member of the Society of Friends throughout her life, or more precisely was considered to be such; her death was officially noted in the Quaker records.[11] The Friends have treated her kindly, and that is as it should be, for throughout her life of devoted service to her adopted country she was certainly at one with them in the spirit if not in the letter. Indeed, as we look at her life we see its light shining not only in her small corner (or two) of St Petersburg, where her contemporaries had reason to be grateful to her, but well beyond, giving us also cause to celebrate her.

From St Petersburg, then, surely following the testimony of Francis William Fox, Richenda Scott refers to affectionate and respectful memories of Sarah at the hospital of the Sisters of Charity.[12] The residents at the Magdalen Institution and the pupils of the Girls' School of Mutual Instruction were of a status making them unlikely to have left records of any such recollections. The same can be said of the women and girls in the later phase of these establishments when she was the director of the Community.

The boarding school fared better than other schools of its type. We have seen that Lancasterian schools had their critics even before the demise of Alexander I. In 1827, under Nicholas I's harsher regime, the climate of suspicion dampened enthusiasm for them and they started rapidly to wither away. Despite claims of cheapness, costs were sometimes a problem too. There had been over 200 of them, and there were still about 213 in 1827, but at the time of Sarah's death a mere handful remained.[13] The Lancasterian school for foreign children was certainly operating in 1854, for Archibald Mirrielees took Robert Charleton and his colleagues there to be shown round.[14] James Heard's son wrote that the Russian Ministry of Education declared the teaching system obsolete and closed the few survivors in 1858.[15] Although we know that Sarah's school weathered this storm under the umbrella of the Community of Sisters of Charity and indeed continued until 1885, apparently with no particular changes,[16] we cannot be sure that it retained its Lancasterian form after her death. She, not her later patrons, had championed that system. What is more important, however, is that the school brought loving care and better prospects to hundreds of girls. As witnesses they are mute but we can be thankful to Sarah on their behalf.

The pioneering character of Sarah's educational and welfare work deserves notice. Although she was certainly not the first person to head a Lancasterian school in Russia, she may well have been the first to run a predominantly residential one on this system for poor girls. She herself claimed to have opened St Petersburg's first infant school in 1831. As for the Magdalens, when Russian historians of medicine and welfare give credit to the German Protestant pastor Theodor Fliedner for organizing a refuge for 'penitent prostitutes' in 1833[17] it is worth remembering that it was in this very same year that Sarah and her friend Mrs Michelson set up a similar home in the Russian capital. The tacit assumption is that they promptly followed suit. Nothing is known about Mrs Michelson's expatriate connections but Sarah was almost certainly aware of developments in Germany through her husband and also her patron the Grand Duchess Elena Pavlovna.

As we look more widely, a legend has had to be discounted but the truth is in many ways more impressive. Nicholas I was not such an admirer of Sarah's administrative prowess that he built a women's hospital for her to manage. One might imagine his brother Alexander doing that, but not him. Instead, however, members of the imperial circle appointed her the first director of a religious order, new to Orthodoxy, whose activities embraced not only the hospital, school and Magdalen home but three other institutions as well. Her responsibilities were far greater than we in her native country have hitherto thought and her role was innovatory. Her influence could still be detected nearly half a century later.[18]

A further reason to pay tribute to Sarah Biller is her role in contributing to and facilitating biography. We may hesitate to call her Hannah Kilham's biographer, for her *Memoir of the Late Hannah Kilham* consists of many long edited extracts from her stepmother's letters and journals, linked by a personal commentary. Sarah is too honest to turn this into hagiography, but family loyalty and affection are too strong for it to be a critical biography either. The loss of the original journals is of course a matter for deep regret; against that, their existence in excerpted form is a considerable consolation. Despite many other carefully collected materials, Mora Dickson could not have written her balanced and objective biography without the building blocks of Sarah's *Memoir*. So it is first of all to Sarah's credit that Hannah's work as a pioneer of African education, missionary and philanthropist did not fall into permanent obscurity. The work of Alison Twells,[19] which convincingly shows Hannah's achievement, suggests moreover that she has won the status of a feminist icon.

It is natural that Sarah's published work should eclipse her other biographical activities, so let us draw attention once more to her important role in supplying fundamental materials to the biographer of her father. She first provided John Blackwell with Alexander Kilham's personal copies of pamphlets which he had written himself or written about, and later sent him his manuscripts and letters. By doing this she was highly instrumental in enabling production of what remains the standard biography of Kilham. It is pleasant to reflect that in Russia she perpetuated his Christian name simply by being herself: the Russian usage of the patronymic – a name derived from one's father's and forming one's middle name – meant that it survived even after her marriage. Thus Sarra Alexandrovna Kil'gam became Sarra Alexandrovna Biller but was known to Russian friends and acquaintances as Sarra Alexandrovna.

Alexander and Hannah Kilham are both celebrated, by connoisseurs at least, for their bravery, independence and strength of character. Her father passed on these qualities to his daughter, and her stepmother encouraged and reinforced them. Sarah occupies a special place among the ranks of British residents in Russia. She did not conform to the usual pattern for young women going there, to be governesses in Russian families. She was a woman in a man's expatriate world. She did not go there, like so many of those men, for commercial reasons. She had no close family there, like some of them, to give her daily support, except while her marriage provided an all too brief respite. She went there from Sheffield with love in her heart for an unknown people, and might be considered primarily naïve, were not her naïvety eclipsed by her courage. She went there, by herself, to enter the Emperor's service and work among his lowliest subjects, and to them she dedicated thirty years of her life. Though she was not a major actor on the stage of history, she deserves to be remembered. We should celebrate our minor heroes too.

Notes and References

1 J.V. Wood, *Some Rural Quakers* (York, 1991), p 128.
2 Worcestershire Record Office (WRO): 8769, 'A Plan of the Meeting House, Grave Yard and other Property belonging to the Society of Friends, Evesham', undated. I should like to thank local Friends for their help, especially Gill Briggs, Warden of the Meeting House at the time of my visit in 2003.
3 Census returns, from: www.ancestrylibrary.com
4 MCL: M85/2/7/1, f 47; M85/2/7/2, f 23; M85/2/8, p 168.
5 MCL: M85/2/7/1, f 47; M85/2/7/2, f 23; M85/2/8, p 196.
6 J. Aitken, ed., *Census of Religious Worship, 1851: The Returns for Worcestershire* ([Worcester,] 2000), p 65.
7 Census returns, from: www.ancestrylibrary.com
8 Cited in Aitken, ed., p 65.
9 WRO: 8769, 'A Plan of the Meeting House...'
10 J. Benson, *Quaker Pioneers in Russia* (1902), pp 94-5.
11 Greenwood, 2, p 145.
12 Scott, p 94.
13 Hollingsworth, p 70.
14 Mason, pp 52, 59.
15 Hollingsworth, p 70, citing I.Ya. Gerd's article on his father in *Russkii biograficheskii slovar'*, vol G-K, p 25.
16 *Istoricheskii ocherk*, p 64.
17 Romanyuk *et al.*
18 *Istoricheskii ocherk*, p 19.
19 A. Twells, '"So Distant and Wild..."'; '"Let us Begin Well..."'; 'The Heathen at Home and Overseas: The Middle Class and the Civilising Mission, Sheffield 1790-1843', PhD thesis, University of York, 1997.

APPENDIX

THE KILHAM FAMILY TREE, SIMPLIFIED

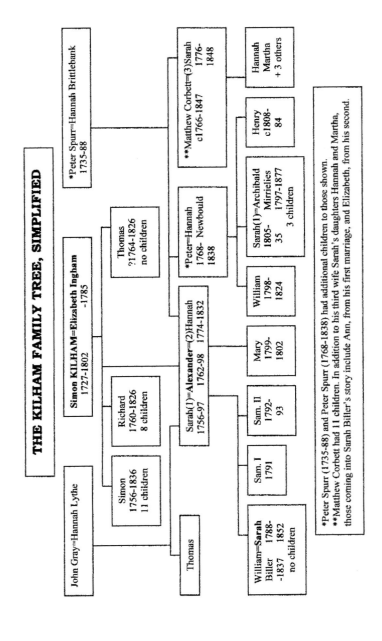

John Gray=Hannah Lythe

*Peter Spurr=Hannah Brittlebank 1735-88

Simon KILHAM=Elizabeth Ingham 1727-1802   -1785

Simon 1756-1836 11 children

Richard 1760-1826 8 children

Thomas ?1764-1826 no children

**Matthew Corbett=(3)Sarah c1766-1847   1776-1848

Thomas

Sarah(1)=Alexander=(2)Hannah 1756-97   1762-98   1774-1832

*Peter=Hannah 1768- Newbould 1838

Hannah Martha + 3 others

William=Sarah Biller 1788--1837   1852 no children

Sam. I 1791

Sam. II 1792-93

Mary 1799-1802

William 1798-1824

Sarah(1)=Archibald 1805-   Mirrielies 35   1797-1877   3 children

Henry c1808-84

*Peter Spurr (1735-88) and Peter Spurr (1768-1838) had additional children to those shown.
**Matthew Corbett had 11 children. In addition to his third wife Sarah's daughters Hannah and Martha, those coming into Sarah Biller's story include Ann, from his first marriage, and Elizabeth, from his second.

135

LIST OF SOURCES

ABBREVIATIONS

BAN	Russian Academy of Sciences Library (also RASL)
BCL	Birmingham Central Library
BFBS	British and Foreign Bible Society
BFSS	British and Foreign School Society
BSA	Bible Society Archives
CUL	Cambridge University Library
CWM	Council for World Mission
FHL	Friends House Library, London
GARF	Main Archive of the Russian Federation, Moscow
GLL	Guildhall Library, London
JRL	John Rylands University Library of Manchester
LA	Lincolnshire Archives, Lincoln
LMS	London Missionary Society
LRA	Leeds Russian Archive, Brotherton Library, University of Leeds
MARC	Methodist Archives and Research Centre
MC	*Manchester Courier*
MCL	Archives and Local Studies, Manchester Central Library
MMER	*The Methodist Magazine, or Evangelical Repository*
MNC	Methodist New Connexion
MNCM	*Methodist New Connexion Magazine and Evangelical Repository*
NIPN	*Novye issledovaniya v pedagogicheskikh naukakh*
NMM	*New Methodist Magazine and Evangelical Repository*
NYRO	North Yorkshire Record Office, Northallerton
PWHS	*Proceedings of the Wesley Historical Society*
RBS	Russian Bible Society
RGIA	Russian State Historical Archive, St Petersburg
SA	Sheffield Archives
SCL	Local Studies Department, Sheffield Central Library
SM	*Sheffield Mercury*
SOAS	School of Oriental and African Studies, University of London
TNA	The National Archives, Kew
WMM	*Wesleyan Methodist Magazine*
WRO	Worcestershire Record Office, Worcester

ARCHIVES

BCL:	Cadbury Collection
CUL:	Bible Society Library, BSA, Foreign Correspondence Inwards, Foreign Correspondence Outwards

CWM: LMS, Russia, Incoming Correspondence; LMS, India and Russia,
        Outgoing Correspondence; LMS, Russia, Richard Knill's Journal
FHL: 033.9664; Dictionary of Quaker Biography; Gibson IV and V;
        Meeting for Sufferings Minutes; Ms 156/123 (Spriggs I); Port D
        and 41; SR 323; Temp Mss
GARF: f.109, op.3, d.2654, copy of *Quatrième rapport*...
GLL: Registers, St Petersburg Anglican Chaplaincy
JRL: Methodist Church Archives (see MARC below)
LA: Quarter Sessions Records; Tonge Collection
LRA: MS 1110, Gellibrand file; MS 1193, Mirrielees file
MARC: MAM PLP; Hobill Collection, Sheffield Deposit
MCL: Census Records; Index to Deeds; Quaker Archives
NYRO: Methodist Membership Lists; Parish Registers and Bishop's
        Transcripts
RGIA: f.1287, op.16, d.1195, file on Benevolent Society of English Ladies
        f.1409, op.2, d.4576, 'Ob uchilishche anglichanki Sarry Kalgam
        dlya bednykh detei zhenskogo pola'
SA: City Archives; Loan Deposits; Parish Registers; Quaker Records
SCL: Census Records (online); Leather's 'Plan of Sheffield'; Tatton Mss
SOAS: Archives of Council for World Mission
TNA: Prob 11/1810, Will of Hannah Kilham
WRO: 8769, Plan of Evesham Friends Meeting House and Burial Ground

Note: The Russian archival citations above have f. for *fond* (group), op. for
opis' (series), and d. for *delo* (file), but are abbreviated in our references.

BOOKS AND ARTICLES

'An Account of Simon Kilham. By his Son', *MMER*, 5 (1802), pp 185-7,
    378-80, 419-22.
ACKROYD, P., *London: The Biography* (London, 2000).
AITKEN, J., ed., *Census of Religious Worship, 1851: The Returns for
    Worcestershire* ([Worcester,] 2000).
*Alfavitnyi ukazatel' imën russkikh deyatelei dlya Russkogo biograficheskogo
    slovarya*, repr. of 1887-88 edn (Nendeln, 1976).
Allen: see Life of William Allen.
AMBLER, R.A., ed., *Lincolnshire Returns of the Census of Religious Worship
    1851*, Lincoln Record Society, 72 ([Lincoln], 1979).
ATKINSON, C., 'Obituary: Mr Simon Kilham', *MNCM*, 40 (1837), pp
    232-4.
ATMORE, C., *The Methodist Memorial* (Bristol, 1801).
BAILEY, F.A., *A History of Southport* (Southport, 1955, repr. 1992).
BAKER, F., 'The Beginnings of Methodism in Lincolnshire', *Journal of the
    Lincolnshire Methodist Historical Society*, 4 (1988), no. 1, pp 4-19.
———— 'Ordinations by Wesley's Preachers', *PWHS*, 24 (1944), pp
    101-2.

BATER, J.H., *St Petersburg: Industrialisation and Change* (London, 1976).
BAZANOV, V., *Uchënaya respublika* (Moscow and Leningrad, 1964).
[BENSON, J.] J.B., *From the Lune to the Neva Sixty Years Ago* (London, 1879).
BENSON, J., *Quaker Pioneers in Russia* (London, 1902).
BILLER, S., ed., *Memoir of the Late Hannah Kilham, Chiefly Compiled from her Journal* (London, 1837).
BILLING, *Directory of Worcestershire* (1855).
BIRRELL, C.M., *The Life of the Rev. Richard Knill, of St Petersburgh*, 3rd edn (London, 1860).
BLACKNER, J., *The History of Nottingham* (Nottingham, 1815).
[BLACKWELL, J.,] anon, *Life of the Rev. Alexander Kilham* (London and Manchester, 1838).
BOWES, H.R., 'Alexander Kilham's Cash Book', *PWHS*, 50 (1996), p 184.
BROKGAUZ, F.A. and EFRON, I.A., *Novyi entsiklopedicheskii slovar'*, 16 (St Petersburg, no date).
BUTLER, D.M., *The Quaker Meeting Houses of Britain*, 2 (London, 1999).
CHAPMAN, S.D., 'The Evangelical Revival and Education in Nottingham', *Transactions of the Thoroton Society of Nottinghamshire*, 66 (1962), pp 35-66.
CLARK, R.H., 'The Steam Engine in Industry and Road Transport', in *Engineering Heritage*, 1 (London, 1963).
DAVIES, T., 'Photos of Eminent Females: Mrs Alexander Kilham', *MNCM*, 89 (1886), pp 83-8.
DICKSON, M., *The Powerful Bond: Hannah Kilham 1774-1832* (London, 1980).
DOLAN, J.A., 'An Independent Methodist Bicentenary', *PWHS*, 50 (1996), pp 237-40.
DUNSTAN, J., 'Alexander's Daughter: The Childhood of Sarah Kilham', *PWHS*, 56 (2008), pp 213-27.
——— *Dore Old School in Records and Recollections* (Sheffield, 2006).
——— 'George A. Simons and the Khristianski Pobornik', *Methodist History*, 19 (1980), pp 21-40.
Editor, The [B. Gregory], 'Alexander Kilham', *WMM*, 6th Series, 11 (1887), pp 689-96, 773-82.
——— 'Were Mr Kilham's Accusations against Wesley, and against his own Fathers and Brethren, true or not?', *WMM*, 6th Series, 12 (1888), pp 458-67, 545-51.
ELLA, C., *Historic Epworth* (Oxford, 1994).
ELLIS, C., *St Peter & St Paul Parish Church, Pickering* (Derby, 2004).
'Extract of a Letter from Mrs Kilham to Mrs Heaps', *MMER*, 2 (1799), pp 329-33.
FON-DER-KHOVEN, I.R., 'Pamyatnik imperatritse Marii Feodorovne', *Russkaya starina*, 9 (1874), pp 203-5.
FORSYTHE, B., 'Venning, John' and 'Venning, Walter', *Dictionary of National Biography*, 56 (Oxford, 2004), pp 265-6 and 267-8.
FOX, A.F., ed., *Memoir of Robert Charleton* (London, 1873).
GALES and MARTIN, *A Directory of Sheffield* (Sheffield, 1787, repr. 1889).

GATTY, A., *Sheffield Past and Present* (Sheffield and London, 1873).

GELL, R., *A New General and Commercial Directory of Sheffield and its Vicinity* (Manchester, 1825).

GIBSON, J., 'Alexander Kilham: A Friendly Review and Reply', *WMM*, 6th Series, 12 (1888), pp 375-81, 445-58.

GORE, *Directory and View of Liverpool and its Environs* (Liverpool, 1834).

Gorodskoi ukazatel' ili adresnaya kniga... na 1850 god (St Petersburg, 1849).

GRAHAM, J.W., 'The Father of the Founder of the "Manchester Guardian"', *Journal of the Friends Historical Society*, 18 (1921), pp 81-7.

GRECH, A., comp., *Ves' Peterburg v karmane* (St Petersburg, 1851).

GREENWOOD, J.O., *Quaker Encounters, 1: Friends and Relief* (York, 1975).

—— *Quaker Encounters, 2: Vines on the Mountains* (York, 1977).

GRUNDELL, J. and HALL, R., ed., *The Life of Mr Alexander Kilham, Methodist Preacher...* [by himself] (Nottingham, 1799).

GÜNTHER, K.-H. *et al.*, *Geschichte der Erziehung* ([East] Berlin, 1987).

HAMM, A., *Der heilige Doktor von Moskau* (Berlin and Bonn, 1979).

Heeley History Workshop, *Heeley and Thereabouts* (Sheffield, 2004).

HENDERSON, T.S., *Memorials of John Venning, Esq.* (London, 1862).

HIBBS, J., *The History of British Bus Services*, 2nd rev. edn (Newton Abbot, 1989).

HINGLEY, R., *The Tsars* (London, 1968, pbk edn 1973).

HOARE, R., *Balby Beginnings: The Launching of Quakerism* (Sheffield, 2002).

[HODGKIN, J., Jr, comp.,] *Extracts from the Familiar Letters of the Late Elizabeth Hodgkin* (London, 1842).

HODGSON, J.S., *A History of Penketh School, 1834-1907* (London, 1907).

HOLLAND, J. and EVERETT, J., *Memoirs of the Life and Writings of James Montgomery*, 7 vols (London, 1854-6).

HOLLINGSWORTH, B., 'Lancasterian Schools in Russia', *Durham Research Review*, 5, no. 17 (1966), pp 59-74.

HOME, G., *The Evolution of an English Town* (London, 1905).

HOWITT, M., *An Autobiography*, 1 (London, 1889).

HUGHES, L., *The Romanovs: Ruling Russia, 1613-1917* (London, 2008).

Isle of Axholme Family History Society, Epworth Parish Registers.

Istoricheskii ocherk Svyato-Troitskoi Obshchiny sestër miloserdiya v S.-Peterburge za pyatidesyatiletie, 1844-1894 (St Petersburg, 1894).

KILHAM, A., *A Short Account of the Life and Death of Mrs Sarah Kilham* (Leeds, 1797).

KILHAM, H., *A Brook by the Way: Extracts from the Diary of Hannah Kilham* (London, 1844).

—— see BILLER, S., ed. and 'Extract of a Letter...'

KILHAM, S., see 'Letter from Miss Kilham...' and 'Religious Intelligence...'

KOPELEW, L., *Der heilige Doktor Fjodor Petrowitsch: die Geschichte des Friedrich Joseph Haass* (Hamburg, 1984).

KUKUSHKIN, V.V., *Toponomika Peterburga-Petrograda...* (St Petersburg, 2000).

LATIMER, R.S., *Russia under Three Tsars* (Kilmarnock, n.d. [latest refs 1909]).

LEADER, R.E., *History of the Company of Cutlers in Hallamshire*, 1 and 2 (Sheffield, 1905-6).
—— ed., *Reminiscences of Old Sheffield* (Sheffield, 1876).
'Letter from Miss Kilham, Daughter of the Late Rev A. Kilham, to her Uncle', *NMM*, 33 (1830), pp 277-8.
Life of William Allen with Selections from his Correspondence, 3 vols (London, 1846-7).
List of the Boys and Girls Admitted into Ackworth School 1779 to 1879 (Ackworth and London, 1879).
LIVINGSTON, J., *Gellibrands* ([Belvedere], 2005).
LOPATINA, E., *Leningrad* (Moscow, 1959).
MAGNITSKY, M.L., 'O vodvorenii illyuminatstva pod raznymi ego vidami v Rossii', in 'Dva donosa v 1831 godu', *Russkaya starina*, 97 (1899), pp 289-314.
MAHNKE-DEVLIN, J., *Britische Migration nach Russland im 19. Jahrhundert* (Wiesbaden, 2005).
MARTIN, A.M., *Romantics, Reformers, Reactionaries* (DeKalb, IL, 1997).
MASON, G.F., *Sleigh Ride to Russia* (York, 1985).
Memoirs of the Life and Gospel Labours of the Late Daniel Wheeler (London, 1842).
MUCKLE, J., *The Russian Language in Britain: A Historical Survey of Learners and Teachers* (Ilkeston, 2008).
MÜLLER-DIETZ, H., *Friedrich Joseph Haass als Arzt in Moskau* (Berlin, 1980).
MYLES, W., *A Chronological History of the People Called Methodists* (1813 edn).
'Ob uchilishche po metode vzaimnogo obucheniya dlya devits', *Sorevnovatel' proshveshcheniya i blagotvoreniya*, 23 (1823), pp 216-18.
OFFICER, L.H., 'Purchasing Power of British Pounds from 1264 to 2007' (2008), from: www.measuringworth.com
OKUN', S.B., *Ocherki istorii SSSR. Konets XVIII – pervaya chetvert' XIX veka* (Leningrad, 1956).
'Ol'denburgskaya printsessa Tereziya-Vil'gel'mina-Frederika-Izabella-Sharlotta', *Biografii Rossiiskikh uchënykh, politikov, literaturnykh deyatelei* (2007), from: www.inform-t.ru/show_bio.aspx_id_100548.php
OSININ, I.T., ed., 'Zapiski kvakera o prebyvanii v Rossii', *Russkaya starina*, 9 (1874), pp 1-36.
PAINA, S.B., 'Peterburgskaya shkola Vol'nogo obshchestva uchrezhdeniya uchilishch vzaimnogo obucheniya (1819-1825)', *NIPN*, 7 (20) (1973), pp 11-13.
—— 'Vol'noe obshchestvo uchrezhdeniya uchilishch vzaimnogo obucheniya (1818-1825 gg.). I. Organizatsiya, sostav i zadachi obshchestva', *NIPN*, 10 (1967), pp 123-7.
—— 'Vol'noe obshchestvo uchrezhdeniya uchilishch vzaimnogo obucheniya (1818-1825 gg.). II. Deyatel'nost' obshchestva', *NIPN*, 12 (1968), pp 104-9.
Pedagogicheskaya entsiklopediya, 1 (Moscow, 1964).

PIGOT & Co., *National Commercial Directory: Manchester* (London and Manchester, 1832).

PITCHER, H., *Muir & Mirrielees* (Cromer, 1994).

PUSHKAREV, S.G., *Obzor russkoi istorii* (New York, 1953).

Quatrième rapport de l'école établie en faveur des enfans [sic] *pauvres parmi les étrangers qui se trouvent à St Pétersbourg pour 1826* (St Petersburg, 1826) (copy in GARF).

'Religious Intelligence: Letter of Miss Kilham, of Russia', *NMM*, 35 (1832), pp 81-2.

ROBERTS, H.E., *Researching Yorkshire Quaker History* (Hull, 2003).

ROBINSON, J., *A Directory of Sheffield* (Sheffield, 1797).

ROMANYUK, V.P., LAPOTNIKOV, V.A. and NAKATIS, Ya.A., 'Istoriya sestrichestva i ukhoda za bol'nymi', *Zolotoi korets* (2004), from: www.randd.ru/Miloserdie_3.htm

ROSE, E.A., 'The First Methodist New Connexion Chapels', *PWHS*, 36 (1967), pp 7-15.

――― 'Kilham, Alexander', in J.A. Vickers, ed., *A Dictionary of Methodism in Britain and Ireland* (Peterborough, 2000), p 191.

――― 'The Methodist New Connexion 1797-1907: Portrait of a Church', *PWHS*, 47 (1990), pp 241-4.

――― 'Sarah Kilham and Hannah Kilham', *PWHS*, 39 (1974), pp 185-6.

ROSSLYN, W., 'Benevolent Ladies and Their Exertions for the Good of Humankind: V.A. Repnina, S.S. Meshcherskaia, and the Origins of Female Philanthropy in Early Nineteenth-Century Russia', *Slavonic and East European Review*, 84 (2006), pp 52-82.

――― 'Women with a Mission: British Female Evangelicals in the Russian Empire in the Early Nineteenth Century', in W. Rosslyn and A. Tosi, ed., *Women in Russian Culture and Society, 1700-1825* (Basingstoke and New York, 2007), pp 219-40.

Rukovodstvo k otyskivaniyu zhilishch po Sanktpeterburgu (St Petersburg, 1824).

RUNICH, D.P., 'Iz zapisok D.P. Runicha', *Russkaya starina*, 106 (1901), pp 373-94.

SAUNDERS, D., *Russia in the Age of Reaction and Reform 1801-1881* (London and New York, 1992).

SCHRADER, T.A., 'Der Beitrag deutscher Ärzte zur Entwicklung der Krankenhäuser in St. Petersburg im 19. Jahrhundert', in I. Kästner and R. Pfrepper, eds, *Medizin und Pharmazie im 18. und 19. Jahrhundert* (Aachen, 2000), pp 129-38.

SCOTT, R.C., *Quakers in Russia* (London, 1964).

SEATON, W., 'Methodism in the Thorne Circuit', *MNCM*, 36 (1833), pp 277-80.

SEEBOHM, B., ed., *Memoirs of the Life and Gospel Labours of Stephen Grellet* (London and Bradford, 1860).

SHEARER, M.M., *Quakers in Liverpool* (Liverpool, 1982).

Sheffield City Libraries, *A Guide to the Fairbank Collection* (Sheffield, 1936).

STEINBERG, R., *Die Anfänge der Strafvollzugsreform in Rußland*... (Frankfurt am Main, 1990).
STEWART, W.A.C., *Quakers and Education* (London, 1953).
STONE, L., *The Family, Sex and Marriage in England 1500-1800*, rev. edn (London, 1979, repr. 1990).
STOTT, A., *Hannah More: The First Victorian* (Oxford, 2003).
'Svyato-Troitskaya obshchina sestër miloserdiya – NII gematologii i transfuziologii' (2008), from: www.citywalls.ru/house3421.html
SWIFT, R.C., 'Hockley Chapel, Nottingham', *PWHS*, 42 (1980), p 123.
——— 'Methodist Sunday Schools in Nottingham', *PWHS*, 33 (1961), pp 17-20, 36-40.
SYKES, J., *The Quakers* (London, 1958).
TAYLOR, J., *Joseph Lancaster: The Poor Child's Friend* (West Wickham, 1996).
THOMAS, R.H.G., *The Liverpool & Manchester Railway* (London, 1980).
TOWNSEND, W.J., *Alexander Kilham, the First Methodist Reformer* (London, n.d. [1889]).
TOWNSEND, W.J., WORKMAN, H.B. and EAYRS, G., *A New History of Methodism*, 2 vols (London, 1909).
TROYAT, H., *Firebrand: The Life of Dostoevsky* (London and Toronto, 1946).
TWELLS, A., '"Let Us Begin Well at Home": Class, Ethnicity and Christian Motherhood in the Writing of Hannah Kilham, 1774-1832', in E.J. Yeo, ed., *Radical Femininity* (Manchester, 1998), pp 25-51.
——— '"So Distant and Wild a Scene": Language, Domesticity and Difference in Hannah Kilham's Writing from West Africa, 1822-1832', *Women's History Review*, 4 (1995), pp 301-18.
'Velikaya knyaginya Elena Pavlovna, 1806-1873', *Russkaya starina*, 33 (1882), pp 781-802.
WALL, G., 'Reminiscences of the Kilham Family', *MNCM*, 52 (1849), pp 126-9.
WALTON, M., *Sheffield: Its Story and its Achievements* (Sheffield, 1948).
WARD, T.A., *Peeps into the Past* (ed. R.E. Leader) (London and Sheffield, 1909).
WARDLE and PRATT, *The Commercial Directory for 1816-17: Rotherham and Sheffield* (Manchester, 1816).
WARE, T., *The Orthodox Church* (Harmondsworth, 1963).
WESLEY, J., *Journal* (ed. N. Curnock) (London, 1915, repr. 1938).
——— *Works, 23: Journal and Diaries VI (1776-86)* (ed. W.R. Ward and R.P. Heitzenrater) (Nashville, TN, 1995).
Wheeler: see Memoirs of the Life...
WHITE, W., *History and General Directory of the Borough of Sheffield* (Sheffield, 1833; 1849-1862).
WILLIAMS, I.A., *The Firm of Cadbury 1831-1931* (London, 1931).
WOOD, J.V., *Some Rural Quakers* (York, 1991).
WYLIE, W.H., *Old and New Nottingham* (London, 1853).
ZACEK, J.C., 'The Lancastrian School Movement in Russia', *Slavonic and East European Review*, 45 (1967), pp 343-67.

NEWSPAPERS AND OTHER SERIALS

The Iris
Manchester Courier
The Methodist Magazine, or Evangelical Repository [MNC 1798-1811]
Methodist New Connexion Magazine [1833-1907]
New Methodist Magazine and Evangelical Repository [MNC 1812-1832]
Novye issledovaniya v pedagogicheskikh naukakh
Proceedings of the Wesley Historical Society
Report of the British and Foreign Bible Society
Report of the British and Foreign School Society
Report of the London Missionary Society
Report of the Sheffield Society for Bettering the Condition and Increasing the Comfort of the Poor
   (from: www.institutions.org.uk/poor_law_unions/sheffield_society)
Russkaya starina
Sheffield Mercury
Wesleyan Methodist Magazine

THESES

DEBONO, L., 'La médecine en Russie de 1801 à 1917' (MD, Université de Franche-Comté, 1997).

MAHNKE-DEVLIN, J., 'Briten in St Petersburg und Moskau im 19. Jahrhundert' (PhD, Ludwig-Maximilians-Universität München, 2002).

TWELLS, A., 'The Heathen at Home and Overseas: The Middle Class and the Civilising Mission, Sheffield 1790-1843' (PhD, University of York, 1997).

WEBSITES

References in brackets are to earlier entries in this List.

www.ancestrylibrary.com
www.citywalls.ru ('Svyato-Troitskaya...')
www.inform-t.ru ('Ol'denburgskaya...')
www.institutions.org.uk (*Report of the Sheffield Society...*)
www.measuringworth.com (OFFICER)
www.randd.ru (ROMANYUK)

INDEX

Abbreviations: AK, Alexander Kilham; dtr, daughter; DW, Daniel Wheeler; fr, father; gfr, grandfather; gmr, grandmother; HK, Hannah Kilham; jr, junior; JV, John Venning; mr, mother; RK, Richard Knill; SB, Sarah Biller; sch(s), school(s); SK, Sarah Kilham; SPB, St Petersburg; sr, senior; WA, William Allen; WB, William Biller.